Gourmet WEEKDAY

< *Fish Fillets with Olives and Oregano, page 106*

Gourmet **WEEKDAY**

All-Time Favorite Recipes

Houghton Mifflin Harcourt
Boston / New York / 2012

Gourmet ® is a registered trademark of Advance Magazine
Publishers, Inc., used under license.

The contents of this book previously appeared in various
issues of *Gourmet* magazine and were published in their
entirety in a special edition of *Gourmet* in September 2010
under the title of *Gourmet Quick Kitchen.*

For information about permission to reproduce selections
from this book, write to Permissions, Houghton Mifflin
Harcourt Publishing Company, 215 Park Avenue South,
New York, New York 10003.

www.hmhbooks.com

Library of Congress Cataloging-in-Publication Data
is available.

ISBN 978-0-547-84231-8

Book design by Margaret Swart

For credits, see page 186.

Printed in the United States of America
DOC 10 9 8 7 6 5 4 3 2 1

CONTENTS

CONTENTS

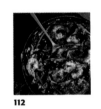

18

20

22

24

26

28

42

44

48

50

52

54

70

72

74

76

78

80

98

102

104

106

108

110

126

128

130

132

134

138

150

154

156

157

158

160

174

176

178

180

182

183

INTRODUCTION

by Sara Moulton

As someone who travels all over the country,

I'm convinced that most people would prefer a homemade meal to fast food during the work week—no matter how quick and easy fast food seems to be. The problem is how to make homemade happen.

If you work regular hours and/or have young children, it often seems as if there's just no time to get a proper dinner on the table. Not true. I'm as pressed as anyone, yet my family enjoys a homemade dinner at least five nights a week because I know how to streamline the menu. My problem is boredom. Like the millions of Americans who do cook, I tend to make the same ten dishes over and over again, simply because doing so requires no thinking.

That's why this little book, *Gourmet Weekday*, with its come-hither photographs, has become such a welcome addition to my kitchen. It's a compilation of the best quick and simple recipes from *Gourmet* magazine, most of them developed by *Gourmet's* food editors, who are everyday people contending with their own hectic lives and family schedules. Unsurprisingly, the recipes are fast and easy. Happily, they are also inspirational—ridiculously simple to make, but special enough to serve at a dinner party, like Crisp Pork Medallions with Caper Sauce or Shrimp and Pancetta on Polenta. They are international (but based on ingredients you can find at the supermarket), seasonal, and budget-friendly.

There are vegetarian recipes, such as Inside-Out Eggplant Parmigiana Stack (a top hit in the *Gourmet* dining room), that won't scare away carnivores; kid-friendly dinners like BLT Burgers that parents will enjoy too; light dishes, such as Fish Fillets with Olives and Oregano, that don't sacrifice flavor; and out-of-the-box weeknight mains—from sandwiches and burgers to pizza, pasta, and rice entrées—guaranteed to shoulder their way into your regular rotation. And that's not even to mention the recipes for knockout desserts. You won't want to miss the decadent Chocolate Fallen Soufflé Cake.

Best of all, more than three-quarters of the recipes in this book take fewer than 30 minutes of hands-on time to prepare. Problem solved: Now you too can serve your family a home-cooked meal any night of the week.

RECIPE TIPS

▶ **MEASURE LIQUIDS** in a glass or clear plastic liquid-measuring cups and **DRY INGREDIENTS** in nesting dry-measuring cups that can be leveled off with a knife.

▶ **MEASURE FLOUR** by spooning (not scooping) it into a dry-measuring cup and leveling off with a knife; do not tap or shake the cup.

▶ **DO NOT SIFT FLOUR UNLESS** specified in the recipe. If sifted flour is called for, sift before measuring. (Disregard "presifted" on the label.)

▶ **SALT:** Measurements are for table salt unless otherwise specified. We don't recommend substituting another type, since the amounts differ when measured by volume.

▶ **BLACK PEPPER** is always freshly ground.

▶ **SPICES:** Store away from heat and light; buy in small quantities.

▶ **TOAST WHOLE SPICES** in a dry heavy skillet over medium heat, stirring, until fragrant and a shade darker, usually 3 to 5 minutes.

▶ **TOAST NUTS** in a shallow baking pan in a 350°F oven until golden, 5 to 15 minutes.

▶ **TOAST SEEDS** like spices or nuts.

▶ **MELT CHOCOLATE** in a metal bowl set over barely simmering water, stirring; or microwave at low to medium power for short intervals (30 seconds or less; stir to check consistency).

▶ **BAKING PANS:** We prefer light-colored metal. If you are using dark metal, including nonstick, your baked goods may brown more, and the cooking times may be shorter. Lower the oven temperature 25°F to compensate.

▶ **NONREACTIVE COOKWARE** includes stainless steel, glass, and enameled cast iron; avoid pure aluminum and uncoated iron, which can impart an unpleasant taste and color to recipes with acidic ingredients.

▶ **WATER BATH FOR BAKING:** Put the filled pan in a larger pan and place in the oven, then add enough boiling water to reach halfway up the side of the smaller pan.

▶ **PRODUCE:** Thoroughly wash and dry all produce before using.

► **GREENS AND CHOPPED/SLICED LEEKS:** Submerge in a large bowl of water, agitating them, then lift out and drain well. If the water in the bowl is dirty, repeat. Pat leeks dry on towels. For greens, spin dry in a spinner several times, stopping to pour off collected water.

► **FRESH HERBS OR GREENS:** Use only the leaves and tender stems.

► **CITRUS ZEST:** Remove the colored part of the rind only (avoid the bitter white pith). For strips, use a vegetable peeler. For grating, we prefer a rasplike Microplane zester, which results in fluffier zest, so pack to measure.

► **CHILES:** Wear protective gloves when handling, and avoid touching your face.

Grilling Procedure

► **CHARCOAL GRILLING INSTRUCTIONS:** Open the vents on the bottom of the grill. Light a large chimney starter full of charcoal.

► **FOR DIRECT-HEAT COOKING:** When the coals are lit, dump them out across the bottom rack, leaving a space free of coals equal to the size of the food to be grilled where you can move the food in case of any flare-ups.

► **FOR INDIRECT-HEAT COOKING:** When the coals are lit, dump them out along two opposite sides of the bottom rack, leaving a space free of charcoal in the middle of the rack equal to the size of the food to be grilled.

► **FOR DIRECT-OR INDIRECT-HEAT COOKING:** When the charcoal turns grayish white, the grill will be at its hottest. How long you can hold your hand 5 inches above the grill rack directly over the coals determines the heat of your grill, as follows:

HOT: 1 to 2 seconds

MEDIUM HOT: 3 to 4 seconds

LOW: 5 to 6 seconds

► **GAS GRILL INSTRUCTIONS**
Preheat all burners on high, covered, for 10 minutes, then adjust the heat according to the recipe. For indirect-heat cooking, just before grilling, turn off one burner (middle burner if there are three).

< Roasted-Tomato Tart, page 22

CHAPTER 1

SNACKS & STARTERS

Meet our favorite attention-getters: snacks, appetizers, and hors d'oeuvres so riotously tasty they'll make the most jaded taste buds snap to attention. A platter of peppery shrimp or a roasted tomato tart can ignite a dinner party the way a great opening scene kick-starts a movie, sharpening everyone's senses and elevating the mood. The lively dishes collected here can also hold their own at a casual get-together, when friends gather to sip wine for an evening. As for how to fit them into a menu, you can match appetizers to one another, or to a meal (serving broccoli rabe crostini before an Italian dinner, say). But you can also use them to provide a taste experience all their own—little snapshots of places you won't otherwise be visiting. Either way, the message comes through: Let the feast begin.

Chile Peanuts

Adapted from Roberto Santibañez

Makes **4 cups** | Active time: **10 minutes** | Start to finish: **1 hour**

Tossed in a lime vinaigrette spiked with spices and then baked till crisp, these are not your average spiced nuts. There's just enough heat from the cayenne to impart a cozy, radiating warmth, while the hit of lime lets them keep their cool.

2½ **tablespoons fresh lime juice**
2 **tablespoons olive oil**
1 **tablespoon paprika (not hot)**
2 **teaspoons fine sea salt**
1 **teaspoon cayenne**
4 **cups unsalted dry-roasted peanuts**

▶ Preheat oven to 250°F, with rack in middle.
▶ Whisk together lime juice, oil, paprika, sea salt, and cayenne. Stir in peanuts to coat evenly.
▶ Spread peanuts on a large baking sheet and bake until coating is dry and fragrant, about 30 minutes. Cool completely before serving.

COOKS' NOTE: Peanuts keep in an airtight container for 3 weeks. If they lose their crispness, reheat in a 250°F oven for 15 to 20 minutes, then cool.

Peaches with Serrano Ham and Basil

Makes **24** | Active time: **15 minutes** | Start to finish: **25 minutes**

3   **peaches, each cut into 8 wedges**
¼   **teaspoon sugar**
½   **teaspoon sherry vinegar**
⅛   **teaspoon ground cumin**
¼   **pound thinly sliced serrano ham**
24   **small basil leaves**

▶ Toss together peaches, sugar, vinegar, and cumin and let stand for 10 minutes.
▶ Cut ham slices in half lengthwise, then wrap each piece around a wedge of peach.
▶ Top with a basil leaf and secure with a wooden or metal pick.

Swaddle a perfectly ripe peach wedge with a silky slice of serrano ham, tucking in a single basil leaf, and you've got yourself an easy and stylish starter that far surpasses the old melon-and-prosciutto standby.

Goat Cheese with Olives, Lemon, and Thyme

Serves **4** | Active time: **10 minutes** | Start to finish: **25 minutes**

File this one under "secret weapon" and pull it out whenever you need a quick but impressive appetizer. Warming the olives in thyme-and-lemon-zest-infused oil awakens their flavor and transforms a goat-cheese medallion into a sumptuous spread.

½ **cup assorted olives**

3 **thyme sprigs**

3 **tablespoons extra-virgin olive oil**

½ **teaspoon grated lemon zest**

¼ **teaspoon black pepper**

1 **(4- to 5-ounce) fresh goat-cheese medallion**
    or 2 (2-ounce) goat-cheese buttons

ACCOMPANIMENT
    Crackers, flatbread, or baguette slices

▸ Heat olives, thyme, oil, zest, and pepper in a small skillet or saucepan over low heat until fragrant (do not simmer). Cool to room temperature.

▸ Pour olive mixture over goat cheese. Serve with crackers, flatbread, or baguette slices.

COOKS' NOTE: This dish can be prepared 2 hours ahead and kept, covered, at room temperature.

Broccoli Rabe Crostini

Adapted from Michele Scicolone

Makes 16 | **Active time: 30 minutes** | **Start to finish: 30 minutes**

A popular side dish, emerald-green broccoli rabe tastes even better as an hors d'oeuvre served on crusty bread. After blanching and a quick sauté, the beautifully wilted stems—still dripping with olive oil and garlic—are piled on little toasts.

KITCHEN TIP
PEEL GARLIC LIKE A PRO

Here's a nifty way to peel a clove without crushing it, for those recipes (like this one) that call for sliced garlic. Hold the top and bottom of a garlic clove between the thumb and forefinger of one hand, then squeeze the clove—use your other hand for added pressure, if necessary—until the skin cracks open. Then start peeling away!

FOR TOASTS

16 (⅓-inch-thick) slices from a 10-inch-long Italian loaf
2 tablespoons olive oil
Salt and black pepper
1 garlic clove, halved crosswise

FOR BROCCOLI RABE TOPPING

1 pound broccoli rabe, tough ends discarded and remainder chopped
2 large garlic cloves, thinly sliced
⅛ teaspoon hot red-pepper flakes
¼ cup olive oil
3 tablespoons water
½ teaspoon salt

▶ **MAKE TOASTS:** Preheat broiler. Put bread slices on a large rimmed baking sheet. Brush both sides of slices with oil, then lightly season with salt and pepper. Broil 4 inches from heat, turning over halfway through broiling, until golden, about 4 minutes total. Rub both sides of toasts with cut sides of garlic (discard garlic).

▶ **MAKE BROCCOLI RABE TOPPING:** Cook broccoli rabe in a 6-quart wide heavy pot of well-salted boiling water, uncovered, until tender, 5 to 6 minutes. Drain well in a colander, gently pressing out excess water. Wipe pot clean.

▶ Cook garlic and red-pepper flakes in oil in pot over moderate heat, stirring occasionally, until garlic is golden, about 2 minutes. Add broccoli rabe, water, and salt and cook, covered, stirring occasionally, 2 minutes.

▶ **ASSEMBLE CROSTINI:** Spoon a heaping tablespoon of warm broccoli rabe topping onto each toast.

COOKS' NOTES: The toasts can be made 1 day ahead and cooled completely, then kept in an airtight container at room temperature.

The broccoli rabe topping can be made 1 day ahead and cooled completely, uncovered, then chilled, covered. Reheat before assembling the crostini.

Avoid bunches of broccoli rabe with bright yellow flowers; they're over-the-hill. As with kale and collards, the prime season is after the first frost, when all three greens explode with sweetness.

Garlic and Cheese Crostini

Makes **24** | Active time: **20 minutes** | Start to finish: **30 minutes**

These toasts are topped with a light sprinkling of minced garlic, olive oil, and sharp Pecorino Romano before being baked. Garlicky and salty, they are a great accompaniment to cocktails.

24 (⅓-inch-thick) baguette slices (from a baguette
     at least 14 inches long)
¼   cup olive oil
¾   cup finely grated Pecorino Romano (preferably
     imported)
5   large garlic cloves, minced
     Kosher salt
¼   teaspoon black pepper
2   tablespoons finely chopped fresh flat-leaf parsley

▶ Preheat oven to 350°F, with rack in middle.

▶ Arrange bread slices in one layer on a large baking sheet and brush tops with 3 tablespoons oil.

▶ Stir together remaining tablespoon oil, cheese, garlic, ¼ teaspoon kosher salt, and pepper in a small bowl.

▶ Sprinkle each slice with about 1 teaspoon cheese mixture, mounding it slightly.

▶ Bake until topping just starts to melt, 6 to 8 minutes. Sprinkle with parsley and kosher salt to taste. Serve warm.

COOKS' NOTE: The cheese mixture can be made 1 day ahead and chilled.

Roasted-Tomato Tart

Serves 6 | Active time: 25 minutes | Start to finish: 1¼ hours

Roasting works magic on tomatoes, concentrating their sweet-tart essence and softening them into an unctuous treat. Perch them on store-bought puff pastry, then scatter with shavings of salty Parmigiano, and you've got a savory tart that may become your most requested recipe.

1   **sheet frozen puff pastry (from a 17¼-ounce package), thawed**

2   **pounds plum tomatoes, halved lengthwise**

2   **tablespoons plus 2 teaspoons extra-virgin olive oil**

3½   **teaspoons finely chopped fresh thyme**

½   **teaspoon salt**
    Black pepper

½   **cup Parmigiano-Reggiano shavings, plus additional for garnish**

▶ Preheat oven to 425°F, with racks in middle and lower third. Line a large baking sheet with foil.

▶ While oven is preheating, roll out pastry sheet on a lightly floured surface with a lightly floured rolling pin into an 11-inch square (⅛ inch thick). Using a plate or pot lid as a guide, cut out a 10-inch round.

▶ Carefully transfer round to an ungreased baking sheet by rolling pastry around rolling pin and then unrolling onto baking sheet. Chill round on baking sheet until ready to use.

▶ Toss tomatoes with 2 tablespoons oil, 2 teaspoons thyme, ¼ teaspoon salt, and ¼ teaspoon pepper in a bowl until well coated. Roast tomatoes, cut sides up and in one layer, in foil-lined baking pan in middle of oven for 1 hour.

▶ Brush pastry round with remaining 2 teaspoons oil, then sprinkle with 1 teaspoon thyme. After roasting tomatoes for 45 minutes, move tomatoes in pan to lower third of oven and put pastry on baking sheet on middle rack.

▶ Bake pastry and tomatoes until pastry is golden brown and puffed and edges of tomatoes are browned but still appear juicy, about 15 minutes.

▶ While pastry is still warm, scatter ½ cup cheese shavings evenly over it. Top shavings with warm tomatoes, cut sides down in an even layer (pastry layers will collapse under tomatoes), then sprinkle evenly with remaining ½ teaspoon thyme, remaining ¼ teaspoon salt, pepper to taste, and additional cheese shavings.

COOKS' NOTE: The tomatoes (without the pastry) can be roasted 1 week ahead and chilled in an airtight container. Reheat in a 350°F oven until heated through before using.

KITCHEN TIP
THE REAL THING

When shopping for Parmigiano-Reggiano, make sure you're getting the genuine article. It's a part-skim cow's-milk cheese artisanally made only in Italy's Emilia-Romagna region and a small area of Lombardy. Production is closely regulated, so look for the words "Parmigiano-Reggiano" stamped on the rind. (If they're not there, you are probably looking at an Italian Grana Padano or an American *grana*, which should be much cheaper.) Buy only what you need, because freshly cut cheese tastes better. Wrap it in cheese paper, wax paper, or parchment paper; plastic wrap will suffocate the product and give it an off flavor. And store it in the crisper drawer of your fridge to keep it moist.

Buckwheat Pancakes with Smoked Salmon

Makes 18 to 20 | **Active time: 25 minutes** | **Start to finish: 25 minutes**

This version of blini is fast because it does not require yeast. If buckwheat flour is unavailable, whole-wheat flour makes a good substitute.

FOR BUCKWHEAT PANCAKES

- ½ **cup all-purpose flour**
- ¼ **cup buckwheat flour**
- 1 **teaspoon sugar**
- ¼ **teaspoon baking soda**
- ¼ **teaspoon salt**
- 2 **large eggs, separated**
- ½ **cup milk**
- 4 **tablespoons (½ stick) unsalted butter, melted**

FOR TOPPING

- ½ **cup sour cream**
- ⅛ **teaspoon salt**
- ⅛ **teaspoon black pepper**
- 1 **teaspoon chopped fresh dill or chives**
- 8 **ounces thinly sliced smoked salmon, cut into small pieces**

GARNISH

Chopped fresh dill or chives

▶ **MAKE PANCAKES:** Whisk together dry ingredients in a large bowl. Whisk together yolks and milk in a small bowl, then whisk into dry ingredients. Beat egg whites in another large bowl with an electric mixer until they hold soft peaks, then fold into flour mixture. Add 3 tablespoons butter and fold until batter is smooth.

▶ Lightly brush a 10- to 12-inch nonstick skillet with some of remaining butter, then heat over moderate heat until hot but not smoking.

▶ Working in batches of 4, spoon about 1½ tablespoons batter per pancake onto skillet and cook until surface of pancakes bubbles, 1 to 2 minutes, then flip and cook for 1 minute more.

▶ Transfer pancakes to a plate and keep warm, covered in foil. Brush skillet with butter between batches.

▶ **MAKE TOPPING:** Stir together all ingredients except salmon until combined, then dollop on pancakes and top each with salmon. Sprinkle with fresh herbs.

COOKS' NOTE: You can substitute 2 ounces of caviar for the smoked salmon.

Mexican Seafood Cocktail

Serves **6** | Active time: **25 minutes** | Start to finish: **25 minutes**

American shrimp cocktail, step aside. This Mexican coastal classic, traditionally served in tall glasses with a spoon, is more like a chunky Virgin Mary: You alternate between fishing out sweet morsels of seafood, onion, and avocado with the spoon and sipping the fragrant liquid.

1½ cups chilled Clamato juice, or 1 cup tomato juice
     and ½ cup bottled clam juice
¼ cup ketchup
¼ cup fresh lime juice
1 teaspoon hot sauce, such as Tabasco
1 teaspoon salt, or to taste
½ cup finely chopped white onion
¼ cup chopped fresh cilantro
1 firm-ripe medium avocado, peeled, pitted,
     and cut into small chunks
½ pound fresh lump crabmeat (1 cup), picked over
¼ pound cooked baby shrimp

ACCOMPANIMENT
     Oyster crackers or saltines (optional)

▶ Stir together Clamato juice, ketchup, lime juice, hot sauce, salt, onion, and cilantro in a large bowl, then gently stir in avocado, crabmeat, and shrimp. Spoon into 6- or 8-ounce glasses or cups. Serve with crackers.

Hot Pepper and Garlic Shrimp

Serves **12** | Active time: **35 minutes** | Start to finish: **35 minutes**

This Spanish tapas favorite, redolent of garlic and packing just the right amount of spicy heat, will disappear fast. It's a recipe you want in your back pocket for those evenings when you have an impromptu gathering of friends and need an easy crowd-pleaser.

- 2 **pounds large shrimp in shell, peeled, leaving tail and first segment of shell intact, and deveined**
- 10 **large garlic cloves, thinly sliced**
- ¼ **teaspoon hot red-pepper flakes**
- ½ **teaspoon fine sea salt**
- ⅓ **cup extra-virgin olive oil**
- 1 **tablespoon fresh lemon juice**

ACCOMPANIMENT
   Lemon wedges

▸ Pat shrimp dry. Cook garlic, red-pepper flakes, and sea salt in oil in a 12-inch heavy skillet over moderately low heat, stirring occasionally, until garlic is pale golden, 4 to 5 minutes. Increase heat to moderately high, then add shrimp and sauté, turning occasionally, until shrimp are just cooked through, 3 to 4 minutes.

▸ Remove from heat and stir in lemon juice, then transfer to a serving bowl. Serve warm or at room temperature with lemon wedges.

KITCHEN TIP
HOW TO DEVEIN A SHRIMP

Deveining shrimp is not an essential step but it's often an aesthetic one. Many cooks skip it for small or medium shrimp, but with larger ones, the "vein"—actually the end of the digestive tract—can sometimes be gritty. The easiest method is to shell the shrimp, then make a shallow cut (about ⅛ inch deep) along the center of the back of the shrimp (the outside curve) with a small, sharp knife to expose the vein. Gently snag the vein with the knife and pull it out, or simply hold the shrimp under running water and rinse it out.

< *Winter Minestrone, page 42*

CHAPTER 2

SOUPS & STEWS

Never underestimate the power of soup. Over and over, just when we think we know everything about it, we come across one that makes us rethink the whole category. The homey but inconsequential soups we grew up with (canned chicken noodle and cream of tomato) have given way to clean, sophisticated purees; remarkable chowders; complexly layered stews that anchor a meal. We've encountered soups that refresh, soups that soothe, and soups that make us want to curl up and read a book. Equally gratifying has been the discovery that freshly made soups needn't spend the better part of a day "developing flavor." In the time it takes to caramelize a few vegetables then simmer until tender, soup can become knock-your-socks-off tasty, and ready to ladle into a waiting bowl.

Spicy Tomato Soup

Serves 4 | **Active time: 20 minutes** | **Start to finish: 40 minutes**

We prefer the taste of organic canned tomatoes in this particular recipe, as they tend to be sweeter. If using other canned tomatoes, you might want to add a bit more sugar to balance their acidity. This soup is delicious with a gooey grilled cheese sandwich.

2   (28- to 32-ounce) cans whole tomatoes in juice (preferably organic)
1   large onion, coarsely chopped
2   teaspoons finely chopped garlic
1   teaspoon finely chopped jalapeño chile, including seeds
2   teaspoons finely chopped peeled fresh ginger
3   tablespoons olive oil
½   teaspoon ground cumin
2¼ cups reduced-sodium chicken broth (18 fluid ounces)
    Sugar and salt

▶ Drain 1 can tomatoes, discarding juice, then puree with remaining can tomatoes (including juice) in a blender.

▶ Cook onion, garlic, chile, and ginger in oil in a 4- to 5-quart heavy nonreactive pot over moderate heat, stirring frequently, until onion is softened, about 8 minutes.

▶ Add cumin and cook, stirring, for 1 minute.

▶ Stir in pureed tomatoes, broth, 1 tablespoon sugar, and 2 teaspoons salt and simmer, uncovered, stirring occasionally, for 20 minutes.

▶ Working in 3 or 4 batches, blend soup in blender until smooth (use caution when blending hot liquids).

▶ Transfer soup as blended to a sieve set over a large bowl and force through sieve, discarding seeds.

▶ Stir in sugar and salt to taste. Reheat in saucepan if necessary.

COOKS' NOTE: The soup can be made 3 days ahead and chilled, covered once cool.

Tomato and Tomatillo Gazpacho

Serves 6 | Active time: 20 minutes | Start to finish: 1½ hours

KITCHEN TIP

TOMATILLOS

Though they resemble husk-covered green tomatoes, these spongy-fleshed fruits are wonderfully tart. Found in Mexico and Guatemala, they're the prime ingredient in salsa verde. Pull the papery husk off before using and rinse the fruit if it's sticky.

This spirited, chunky gazpacho in the Mexican mode is a warm-weather favorite. Tomatoes give the soup a rich, rounded flavor, and tomatillos—an Aztec and Mayan staple—lend fruity tartness and great body.

½ pound fresh tomatillos, husked, rinsed, and quartered
1½ pounds tomatoes, chopped
½ cup chopped white onion
1 serrano chile, coarsely chopped, including seeds
1 garlic clove, quartered
2 tablespoons red-wine vinegar
1¼ teaspoons salt
1 cup water
2 tablespoons olive oil
½ cup chopped fresh cilantro

▶ Puree tomatillos, half of tomatoes, and half of onion with chile, garlic, vinegar, and salt in a blender until smooth.
▶ Force through a medium-mesh sieve into a bowl, discarding solids.
▶ Stir in remaining tomatoes and onion, water, oil, and cilantro.
▶ Chill until cold, at least 1 hour and up to 4 hours.

Fast White-Bean Stew

Serves 4 | Active time: **10 minutes** | Start to finish: **20 minutes**

A colorful and satisfying stew is priceless any time of year, and you can't do much better than a tomatoey broth full of hearty cannellini beans, baby greens, and chunks of baked ham.

2   large garlic cloves, chopped
¼   cup plus ½ tablespoon extra-virgin olive oil
1   (14- to 15-ounce) can stewed tomatoes
1¾ cups reduced-sodium chicken broth
2   (19-ounce) cans cannellini beans, rinsed and drained (3 cups)
1   (½-pound) piece baked ham (½ inch to ¾ inch thick), cut into ½-inch chunks
¼   teaspoon black pepper
1   (5-ounce) bag baby romaine or baby arugula (10 cups loosely packed)
8   (¾-inch-thick) slices baguette

▶ Cook garlic in ¼ cup oil in a 4- to 5-quart heavy pot over moderately high heat, stirring, until golden, 1 to 2 minutes.

▶ Coarsely cut up tomatoes in can with kitchen shears, then add (with juice) to garlic in oil. Stir in broth, beans, ham, and pepper and bring to a boil.

▶ Reduce heat and simmer, uncovered, for 5 minutes. Stir in greens and cook until wilted, 3 minutes for romaine or 1 minute for arugula.

▶ While stew is simmering, preheat broiler.

▶ Put bread on a baking sheet and drizzle with remaining ½ tablespoon oil. Broil 3 to 4 inches from heat until golden, 1 to 1½ minutes.

▶ Serve stew with toasts.

Curried Squash and Red-Lentil Soup

Serves **4 to 6** | Active time: **25 minutes** | Start to finish: **1¼ hours**

Sweet butternut squash, earthy red lentils, and curry powder are the stars of this lively vegetarian soup that's wonderful ladled over basmati rice. A drizzle of cilantro oil heightens the wow factor.

- 3 **tablespoons vegetable oil**
- 2 **tablespoons unsalted butter**
- 1½ **pounds butternut squash, peeled and cut into ½-inch pieces**
- 1 **large onion, chopped**
- 1 **carrot, chopped**
- 1 **celery rib, chopped**
- 2 **garlic cloves, minced**
- 2 **tablespoons minced peeled fresh ginger**
  Salt
- 1 **tablespoon curry powder (preferably Madras)**
  Black pepper
- 1 **cup red lentils, picked over and rinsed**
- 2 **quarts water**
- 1 **teaspoon fresh lemon juice, or to taste**
- ½ **cup chopped fresh cilantro**
- ½ **cup vegetable oil**

ACCOMPANIMENT
  Cooked basmati rice

▶ Heat oil with butter in a large heavy pot over medium heat until foam subsides, then cook squash, onion, carrot, celery, garlic, ginger, and 1 teaspoon salt, stirring occasionally, until vegetables are softened and beginning to brown, 15 to 20 minutes.

▶ Stir in curry powder and ¼ teaspoon pepper and cook, stirring frequently, for 2 minutes.

▶ Add lentils and water and simmer, covered, until lentils are tender, 25 to 40 minutes. Stir in lemon juice and season with salt and pepper.

▶ Puree cilantro, oil, and ½ teaspoon salt in a blender.

▶ Serve soup over rice, drizzled with cilantro oil.

COOKS' NOTE: The soup, without the cilantro oil, can be made 3 days ahead and chilled.

KITCHEN TIP
HOW TO CHOP BUTTERNUT SQUASH

Of all the winter squashes, the butternut is the easiest to peel and cut up. When shopping, select one with a large neck. Trim off the top and bottom of the squash with a large sharp knife. Cut the neck free from the bulbous section (where the seeds are), then slice it crosswise into thick rounds (1½ to 2 inches). Working with each round flat on the cutting board, trim off the skin with the knife, rotating the round as you go. Next, stand the bulbous section on its base and halve it lengthwise. Scoop out the seeds and reserve them (they are delicious toasted and salted), then cut the halves crosswise into 1½- to 2-inch sections. Place each section on a cut side and trim off the skin with the knife. (A sharp vegetable peeler could work, but if the skin is really thick, a peeler can be frustrating.) Once all the squash is peeled, you can chop the rounds into pieces.

Portuguese Kale and Potato Soup

Serves **4** | Active time: **15 minutes** | Start to finish: **45 minutes**

The Portuguese soup *caldo verde* is ideal cool-weather comfort food. It's full of good-for-you greens and potatoes, while sausage keeps things meaty and satisfying.

¼ cup extra-virgin olive oil
½ pound chouriço or linguiça (smoked Portuguese sausages) or kielbasa, cut into ½-inch pieces
1 medium onion, chopped
2 garlic cloves, minced
  Salt and black pepper
1 pound russet (baking) potatoes, peeled and cut into 1-inch pieces
6 cups water
1 pound kale, stems and center ribs discarded and leaves very thinly sliced

ACCOMPANIMENT
  Piri-piri sauce or other hot sauce

▶ Heat 1 tablespoon oil in a 5-quart heavy pot over medium-high heat until it shimmers, then brown sausage, stirring often, for 2 to 3 minutes. Transfer with a slotted spoon to a bowl.
▶ Add 2 tablespoons oil to fat in pot and cook onion and garlic with ¼ teaspoon each salt and pepper over medium heat, stirring often, until browned, 7 to 8 minutes.
▶ Add potatoes, water, and 1 teaspoon salt and simmer, covered, until potatoes are very tender, 15 to 20 minutes.
▶ Mash some potatoes into soup to thicken, then add kale and simmer, uncovered, until tender, about 5 minutes.
▶ Stir in sausage and cook until just heated through, 1 to 2 minutes.
▶ Drizzle with remaining tablespoon oil and season with salt and pepper. Serve with hot sauce.

COOKS' NOTE: The soup can be made 2 days ahead and chilled, covered, once cool. Although the kale will lose its vibrant green color, the soup will improve in flavor. Reheat slowly, uncovered, thinning with additional water if necessary.

Zucchini-Basil Soup

Serves **4 to 6** | Active time: **30 minutes** | Start to finish: **45 minutes**

This smooth pureed soup manages the near-impossible feat of being velvety and creamy without any cream. Ribbons of zucchini add a final elegant note.

2 **pounds zucchini, trimmed and cut crosswise into thirds**

Salt

¾ **cup chopped onion**

2 **garlic cloves, chopped**

¼ **cup olive oil**

4 **cups water**

⅓ **cup packed fresh basil leaves**

Black pepper

SPECIAL EQUIPMENT

Mandoline or other adjustable-blade slicer fitted with ⅛-inch julienne attachment

▶ Julienne skin (only) from half of zucchini with slicer, then toss it with ½ teaspoon salt and drain in a sieve until wilted, at least 20 minutes.

▶ Meanwhile, coarsely chop remaining zucchini. Cook onion and garlic in oil in a 3- to 4-quart heavy saucepan over medium-low heat, stirring occasionally, until softened, about 5 minutes.

▶ Add chopped zucchini and 1 teaspoon salt and cook, stirring occasionally, for 5 minutes.

▶ Add 3 cups water and simmer, partially covered, until tender, about 15 minutes.

▶ Add basil leaves and puree soup in 2 batches in a blender (use caution when blending hot liquids).

▶ Bring remaining cup water to a boil in a small saucepan and blanch julienned zucchini for 1 minute. Drain in a sieve set over a bowl (use liquid to thin soup if necessary).

▶ Season soup with salt and pepper.

▶ Serve in shallow bowls with julienned zucchini mounded on top.

COOKS' NOTE: The soup and the julienned zucchini garnish can be made 2 days ahead. Chill the soup, covered, once cool. Cool the zucchini garnish completely, uncovered, before chilling, covered. Bring the garnish to room temperature for serving. This soup is delicious hot or cold.

Winter Minestrone

Serves 8 | **Active time: 45 minutes** | **Start to finish: 2 hours**

This soul-satisfying soup is easy to make, but requires some hands-off cooking time. Don't worry about prepping all your vegetables before you begin—you can simply chop as you go.

KITCHEN TIP

FLAVOR TECHNIQUE

The deep, full taste of this stick-to-your-ribs soup comes from the *soffritto*—a mixture of pancetta, onion, celery, carrots, and chard ribs—and from browning the tomato paste. The result is so savory that there's no need for broth: Water, canned tomatoes, and a Parmesan rind work beautifully.

⅓ pound sliced pancetta, chopped

3 medium red onions, chopped

4 celery ribs, chopped

2 medium carrots, chopped

⅓ cup extra-virgin olive oil

1 bunch Swiss chard

6 garlic cloves, finely chopped
Salt and black pepper

2 tablespoons tomato paste

1 (28-ounce) can whole tomatoes in juice

3 quarts hot water

5 cups coarsely chopped cored Savoy cabbage

5 cups coarsely chopped escarole

1 piece Parmigiano-Reggiano rind (about 3 inches by 1 ½ inches)

1 (19-ounce) can cannellini beans, rinsed and drained

ACCOMPANIMENTS
Extra-virgin olive oil for drizzling; cooked ditalini pasta tossed with oil (optional); grated Parmigiano-Reggiano

▶ Cook pancetta, onions, celery, and carrots in oil in a wide 7- to 9-quart heavy pot over medium heat, stirring occasionally, while preparing chard.

▶ Cut out stems from chard and chop stems, reserving leaves.

▶ Stir chard stems into pancetta mixture with garlic, 1 teaspoon salt, and ¾ teaspoon pepper (set aside chard leaves).

Continue cooking, stirring occasionally, until vegetables are very tender and begin to stick to bottom of pot, about 45 minutes total.

▶ Push vegetables to one side of pot. Add tomato paste to cleared area and cook, stirring constantly, until it starts to caramelize, about 2 minutes.

▶ Stir paste into vegetables and cook, stirring, for 2 minutes. (Paste may stick to pot, but don't let it burn.)

▶ Stir in tomatoes with their juice, breaking them up with a spoon, then add the hot water, scraping up any brown bits from bottom of pot.

▶ Bring to a simmer. Stir in cabbage, escarole, and Parmesan rind. Simmer, covered, until greens are tender, about 40 minutes.

▶ Coarsely chop chard leaves and stir into soup along with beans.

▶ Simmer, partially covered, for 10 minutes. Discard Parmesan rind.

▶ Season soup with salt and pepper. If using ditalini, stir in just before serving. Pass olive oil, cooked pasta, and Parmesan at the table.

COOKS' NOTE: Soup, without pasta, can be made 2 days ahead and chilled.

Shellfish Chowder

Serves **4** | Active time: **20 minutes** | Start to finish: **40 minutes**

Shrimp, scallops, and lobster mingle amiably with diced potatoes and a little smoky bacon in this New England–style shellfish chowder enlivened with cilantro and chives. Feel free to vary the mix and proportions of the shellfish, depending on what you find at the market.

5   **bacon slices, finely chopped**
2   **boiling potatoes (¾ pound total), cut into ¼-inch dice**
½   **cup finely chopped shallots (2 large)**
¾   **cup bottled clam juice**
2½   **cups whole milk**
⅛   **teaspoon cayenne**
¼   **pound shrimp, shelled, deveined, and cut into ½-inch pieces**
½   **pound sea scallops, quartered and tough ligament removed from side of each if necessary**
1   **teaspoon salt**
½   **pound shelled cooked lobster meat, cut into ½-inch-thick pieces, or ½ pound lump crabmeat, picked over**
2   **tablespoons chopped fresh cilantro**
2   **tablespoons chopped fresh chives**

▶ Cook bacon in a 5-quart heavy pot over moderate heat, stirring occasionally, until crisp, about 5 minutes.
▶ Transfer bacon with a slotted spoon to paper towels to drain.
▶ Pour off all but 1 tablespoon fat from pot and stir in potatoes, shallots, and clam juice. Simmer, covered, until potatoes are tender, about 8 minutes.
▶ Stir in milk and cayenne and return just to a simmer.
▶ Add shrimp, scallops, and salt and simmer, stirring occasionally, until shellfish is just cooked through, 3 to 5 minutes.
▶ Stir in lobster or crabmeat and half of herbs and simmer for 1 minute.
▶ Serve chowder topped with bacon and remaining herbs.

< *Lobster Rolls,*
page 52

CHAPTER 3

SANDWICHES & BURGERS

Rich lobster salad, molten Taleggio cheese, Latin-spiced black-bean burgers—none would taste quite as good without the comforting ballast of bread and its kin (rolls, buns, baguettes). Sandwiches and burgers are prized by cooks as a speedy, effortless way to satisfy a diverse crowd, allowing everyone to customize their own fillings and toppings—adding or removing ingredients, blending condiments, moving things around to get the right combination in each bite. But we suspect that the real key to their popularity is primal: We eat them with our hands.

Grilled Cheese with Onion Jam, Taleggio, and Escarole

Serves **2** | Active time: **15 minutes** | Start to finish: **15 minutes**

Here's a grilled cheese sandwich with personality: Creamy Italian Taleggio is balanced by the savory sweetness of onion jam and tempered by the slight bitterness of wilted escarole. Sourdough bread provides just the right amount of crunchy support.

4 (½-inch-thick) center slices sourdough bread (from a 9- to 10-inch round)
4 teaspoons extra-virgin olive oil
1½ tablespoons onion or fig jam
12–14 ounces chilled Taleggio or Italian Fontina, sliced
¼ pound escarole, center ribs discarded and leaves cut crosswise into 1-inch pieces (about 2 cups)
Salt and black pepper

▶ Brush 1 side of bread slices with oil and arrange, oil sides down, on a work surface. Spread jam on 2 slices of bread and divide cheese between remaining 2 slices.

▶ Mound escarole on top of cheese and season with salt and pepper, then assemble sandwiches.

▶ Heat a dry 12-inch heavy skillet (not nonstick) over medium-low heat until hot. Cook sandwiches, turning once and pressing with a spatula to compact, until bread is golden brown and cheese is melted, 6 to 8 minutes total.

KITCHEN TIP
TALEGGIO CHEESE

A deep, experimental sniff of a Taleggio from Lombardy, one of the world's great aromatic cheeses, yields a tantalizing blend of rich cow's milk, damp loam, and sweet, fresh hay. In taste, the cheese is nutty and surprisingly mild, with a fruity tang; its texture ranges from elastic to creamy.

Black-Bean Burgers

Serves **4** | Active time: **10 minutes** | Start to finish: **15 minutes**

There are lots of meatless burgers in the world, but this one—earthy and satisfying without being stodgy—has Latino flair and is pantry-friendly, to boot.

2 (14-ounce) cans black beans, rinsed and well drained
3 tablespoons mayonnaise
⅓ cup plain dry bread crumbs
2 teaspoons ground cumin
1 teaspoon dried oregano, crumbled
¼ teaspoon cayenne
¼ cup finely chopped fresh cilantro
3 tablespoons vegetable oil
4 soft hamburger buns

ACCOMPANIMENTS
Sour cream; salsa; lettuce

▶ Pulse 1 can beans in a food processor with mayonnaise, bread crumbs, cumin, oregano, and cayenne until a coarse puree forms. Transfer to a bowl and stir in cilantro and remaining can beans. Form mixture into 4 patties.

▶ Heat oil in a 12-inch heavy skillet over medium-high heat until it shimmers. Cook burgers until outsides are crisp and lightly browned, turning once, about 5 minutes total. Serve on buns with accompaniments.

Lobster Rolls with Lemon Vinaigrette and Garlic Butter

Serves 6 | **Active time: 25 minutes** | **Start to finish: 50 minutes**

We've lightened up a classic by replacing the mayonnaise with a fresh lemon vinaigrette that doesn't mask the sweet flavor of the lobster. The other unorthodox touch is the garlic-buttered bun. If you want to skip the bread, the lobster would make an ideal centerpiece in a summer salad.

- 4 (1¼- to 1½-pound) live lobsters
- 3 tablespoons fresh lemon juice
- ⅓ cup extra-virgin olive oil
  Salt
- ⅓ cup thinly sliced scallions
- ¼ cup finely chopped peeled celery
- ¼ cup chopped celery leaves
- ¼ cup chopped fresh flat-leaf parsley
- 4 tablespoons (½ stick) unsalted butter
- 3 garlic cloves, smashed
- 6 hot dog buns

ACCOMPANIMENT
  Lemon wedges

▶ Prepare a gas grill for direct-heat cooking over medium-high heat; see "Grilling Procedure," page 11.

▶ Plunge 2 lobsters headfirst into a large pot of salted boiling water and cook, partially covered, over medium-high heat for 8 minutes (for 1¼-pound lobsters) to 9 minutes (for 1½-pound lobsters) from time they enter water. Transfer with tongs to an ice bath and let stand until completely cooled. Return water to a boil and cook and cool remaining 2 lobsters. Remove meat from claws, joints, and tails. Coarsely chop meat.

▶ Whisk together lemon juice, oil, and ½ teaspoon salt in a large bowl. Whisk in scallions, celery, celery leaves, and parsley, then add lobster and gently toss. Season with salt.

▶ Melt butter with garlic in a small saucepan over low heat, mashing garlic with a spoon.

▶ Brush inside of buns with garlic butter. Grill, buttered side down, until golden, about 1 minute. Fill buns with lobster.

▶ Serve with lemon wedges.

COOKS' NOTES: The lobsters can be cooked 1 day ahead. Remove the meat from shells and chill.

The buns can be grilled in a lightly oiled hot two-burner grill pan over medium heat or toasted in a 350°F oven for 5 to 7 minutes.

KITCHEN TIP
HOW TO COOK LOBSTER

As tempting as it might be to save time by putting all four lobsters in the pot at once, we urge you to hold off and do as we suggest in the recipe, just 2 at a time. Why, you ask? Because it's easy to screw up cooking a lobster: It doesn't give many clues as to when it's finished. The shell turns red before the meat is done, so you can't use color as a guide. For tender cooked meat, we based our timing on an 8-quart pot two-thirds to three-fourths filled with salted boiling water—a size that many cooks have, particularly if they cook pasta. If you were to add more than the two lobsters called for, the temperature of the water would drop precipitously and the timing would be off. So sit down and pour yourself another glass of wine and enjoy the extra 8 to 9 minutes.

BLT Burgers

Serves **4** | Active time: **25 minutes** | Start to finish: **50 minutes**

With the exception of beef and cheese, there's no burger combination more revered than beef and bacon. Here, we've improved on a classic by putting crumbled bacon in the middle. It adds unexpected bits of crisp texture and diffuses smoky flavor throughout the beef.

½ **pound bacon, sliced**
1½ **pounds lean ground beef chuck**
   Salt and black pepper
4 **hamburger buns, split and grilled**
ACCOMPANIMENTS
   Mayonnaise; mustard; iceberg lettuce;
   sliced tomatoes; dill pickles

▶ Cook bacon in a 12-inch heavy skillet over medium heat, stirring occasionally, until crisp, then transfer with a slotted spoon to paper towels to drain. Cool to room temperature, about 5 minutes.

▶ Holding one fourth of beef in your palm, make a depression in beef and add one fourth of bacon to depression. Pull beef over bacon to enclose completely, then flatten into a ¾-inch-thick patty (4 inches in diameter). Make 3 more patties in same manner with remaining beef and bacon.

▶ Prepare grill for direct-heat cooking over medium-hot charcoal (medium heat for gas); see "Grilling Procedure," page 11.

▶ Season patties on both sides with salt and pepper. Oil grill rack, then grill patties, covered only if using a gas grill, turning over once, 5 to 8 minutes total for medium-rare. (Burgers will continue to cook slightly after being removed from grill.)

▶ Assemble burgers with buns and accompaniments.

COOKS' NOTES: The patties can be formed up to 1 hour ahead and chilled, covered.

If you aren't able to grill outdoors, you can sauté patties in 3 tablespoons bacon fat remaining in skillet (discard remainder) over medium-high heat, turning over once, 6 to 8 minutes for medium-rare.

KITCHEN TIP
OF BACON AND BURGERS

Everyone has their favorite bacon, but when it's cooked, crumbled, and embedded inside a ground-beef patty, you want a bacon that will stand up and be noticed. This is the time to go for a seriously smoky flavor: applewood-smoked, cob-smoked, or even double-smoked bacon. When forming burgers from ground meat, the general rule is to handle the beef as gently as possible to keep it from getting tough. Even though in this recipe you've got to work with each patty in order to stuff it, aim to do so with the minimal amount of prodding and pressing.

Sophisto Joes

Serves **4** | Active time: **25 minutes** | Start to finish: **35 minutes**

These are the Cary Grants of sloppy joes—suavely seasoned with red wine, tomatoes, Worcestershire, and a mirepoix of onion, carrot, and celery (as opposed to ketchup and green peppers), yet right at home at the kitchen table with a glass of beer.

1 (14- to 15-ounce) can whole tomatoes in juice, drained
1 large onion, chopped
4 garlic cloves, finely chopped
2 tablespoons unsalted butter
1 medium carrot, finely chopped
1 celery rib, finely chopped
  Salt
1½ pounds ground beef chuck
1 tablespoon chili powder
1 teaspoon ground cumin
  Black pepper
½ cup dry red wine
2 tablespoons Worcestershire sauce
1½ tablespoons packed brown sugar
4 kaiser rolls, split

▶ Puree tomatoes in a blender.
▶ Cook onion and garlic in butter in a 12-inch heavy skillet over medium-high heat, stirring occasionally, until onion begins to brown, 4 to 5 minutes. Add carrot, celery, and ½ teaspoon salt and cook, stirring occasionally, until vegetables are softened, 4 to 5 minutes.
▶ Add beef and brown, stirring to break up lumps, 5 to 6 minutes. Add chili powder, cumin, ½ teaspoon salt, and ¾ teaspoon pepper and cook, stirring, for 2 minutes. Add pureed tomatoes, wine, Worcestershire sauce, and brown sugar and boil, stirring occasionally, until sauce has thickened, about 6 minutes.
▶ Season with salt and pepper, then sandwich inside rolls.

Banh Mi

Serves **4** | Active time: **30 minutes** | Start to finish: **30 minutes**

Despite the exotic name of this sandwich, you can get all the ingredients right at the supermarket. Liverwurst stands in for the traditional pork pâté filling—the meatiness works beautifully with the sharp-flavored vegetables and fresh cilantro.

½ pound daikon, peeled
1 carrot, peeled
½ cup rice vinegar (not seasoned)
1 tablespoon sugar
½ teaspoon salt
1 (24-inch) soft baguette
2 tablespoons vegetable oil
1 tablespoon Asian fish sauce
½ teaspoon soy sauce
¼ pound liverwurst
2 jalapeño chiles, thinly sliced
½ sweet onion, cut into ¼-inch-thick rings
¾ cup packed cilantro sprigs
2 cooked chicken breasts from a rotisserie chicken, thinly sliced
Lettuce leaves
2 tablespoons mayonnaise

▶ Preheat oven to 350°F, with rack in middle.
▶ Shred daikon and carrot in a food processor fitted with medium shredding disk.
▶ Stir together vinegar, sugar, and salt and toss with shredded vegetables. Let slaw stand, stirring occasionally, for 15 minutes.
▶ Meanwhile, heat baguette on rack in oven until crusty, about 5 minutes. Cut off and discard round ends, then split baguette lengthwise.
▶ Mix together oil, fish sauce, and soy sauce and brush on cut sides of bread. Spread liverwurst on bottom layer of bread and top with chiles, onion, and cilantro.
▶ Drain slaw in a colander.
▶ Arrange chicken, slaw, and lettuce on cilantro. Spread top layer of bread with mayonnaise and cut sandwich crosswise into fourths.

Barbecued Pork Burgers with Slaw

Serves **4** | Active time: **25 minutes** | Start to finish: **50 minutes**

Spicing up store-bought barbecue sauce with cayenne and vinegar is an easy trick that makes a big difference. Here, the sauce is mixed into the meat, slathered onto the cooked burgers for the last minute of grilling, and brushed on the bun.

¼ cup mayonnaise
1 tablespoon milk
1½ tablespoons white-wine vinegar
2 cups thinly sliced green cabbage
½ cup very finely shredded carrot
1 tablespoon thinly sliced fresh chives
   Salt and black pepper
½ cup bottled tomato-based barbecue sauce
¼ teaspoon cayenne
1½ pounds ground pork
4 kaiser or soft rolls, split and grilled

▶ Prepare grill for direct-heat cooking over medium-hot charcoal (medium heat for gas); see "Grilling Procedure," page 11.
▶ Whisk together mayonnaise, milk, and 1½ teaspoons vinegar until smooth, then toss with cabbage, carrot, chives, and salt and pepper to taste. Let coleslaw stand at room temperature, uncovered, while making burgers.
▶ Stir together barbecue sauce, cayenne, ¼ teaspoon salt, and remaining tablespoon vinegar until combined.
▶ Mix together pork, ½ teaspoon salt, ¼ teaspoon pepper, and 2 tablespoons barbecue sauce mixture until combined (do not overmix), then form into 4 (¾-inch-thick) burgers (4 inches in diameter).
▶ Oil grill rack, then grill patties, covered only if using a gas grill, turning over occasionally, until just cooked through, about 6 minutes total. Brush top of each patty with 1 tablespoon barbecue sauce mixture, then turn over and grill for 30 seconds. Repeat with other side.
▶ Brush cut sides of rolls with remaining ¼ cup barbecue sauce, then assemble burgers with rolls and coleslaw.

COOKS' NOTE: The coleslaw can be made 8 hours ahead and chilled, covered.

KITCHEN TIP
BUYING GROUND PORK

Although most of the ground pork that you buy in the supermarket doesn't indicate what part of the pig it hails from, we know that a good pork burger—like a good beef burger—is made from shoulder meat. If you have access to a butcher, ask for your pork to be ground from the shoulder (ideally the pork butt, a confusingly named shoulder cut). It's got a good ratio of meat to fat, and for a juicy, flavorful burger, lean is not the way to go; fat is where the real flavor is. For the best texture, ask the butcher to run it through the grinder only once, on a coarse setting.

CHAPTER 4

PASTA, PIZZA & RICE

How do we love pasta, pizza, and rice? We stopped counting the ways a decade ago, when the anti-carb evangelists compelled us to deny our affection. These days, we're happy to admit we adore them all, and express our feelings unabashedly all year round—tossing angel hair with fresh tomatoes in summer, and fettuccine with sausage and kale when the weather turns cold. These staples are so easy to cook, and so readily combined with just about anything else on hand, that security for us has come to mean a freezer full of premade pizza dough or a pantry shelf piled with bags of pasta and rice in all shapes and fragrant varieties. In little more than the time it takes to bake a saucy crust or boil a pot of water, dinner is served.

Pizza Margherita

Serves 4 | **Active time: 20 minutes** | Start to finish: **1 hour**

The secret to a great pizza Margherita is to use the best ingredients you can find—and to approach them with restraint. To save time, we've started with store-bought dough, the perfect canvas for bright homemade tomato sauce, fresh mozzarella, and verdant basil leaves.

KITCHEN TIP

WORKING WITH DOUGH

In this age of do-it-yourself everything, don't feel guilty about using store-bought pizza dough when you're pinched for time. It's a perfectly acceptable substitute for homemade. Just make sure that the frozen dough thaws to room temperature before you begin, and resist the urge to punch it down or knead it briefly. The dough will be much easier to work with, and it will make for a lighter crust with more of those delightful blistery bubbles of bread, sauce, and cheese.

1 (14- to 15-ounce) can whole tomatoes in juice
2 large garlic cloves, smashed
2 tablespoons olive oil
4 basil leaves, plus more for sprinkling
¼ teaspoon sugar
Salt
1 pound pizza dough, thawed to room temperature if frozen
Unbleached all-purpose flour for dusting dough
6 ounces fresh mozzarella, cut into ¼-inch-thick slices

SPECIAL EQUIPMENT
Pizza stone

▶ **HEAT PIZZA STONE:** Put stone on oven rack in lower third of electric oven (or on floor of gas oven) and preheat oven to 500°F. (This can take as long as 45 minutes.)

▶ **MAKE TOMATO SAUCE WHILE PIZZA STONE IS HEATING:** Pulse tomatoes with juice in a blender briefly to make a chunky puree.

▶ Cook garlic in oil in a small heavy saucepan over medium-low heat until fragrant and pale golden, about 2 minutes. Add tomato puree, basil, sugar, and ⅛ teaspoon salt and simmer, uncovered, stirring occasionally, until thickened and reduced to about 1 cup, 30 to 40 minutes. Remove from heat and season with salt.

▶ **SHAPE DOUGH WHILE SAUCE IS SIMMERING:** Dust dough with flour, then transfer to a parchment-lined pizza peel or large baking sheet. Pat out dough evenly with your fingers and stretch into a 14-inch round, reflouring fingers if necessary.

▶ **ASSEMBLE PIZZA:** Spread sauce over dough, leaving a 1-inch border (there may be some sauce left over). Arrange cheese on top, leaving a 2- to 3-inch border.

▶ Slide pizza on parchment onto pizza stone. Bake until dough is crisp and browned and cheese is golden and bubbling in spots, 12 to 16 minutes. Using peel or baking sheet, transfer pizza to a cutting board. Cool for 5 minutes. Sprinkle with some basil leaves before slicing.

COOKS' NOTE: The tomato sauce can be made 5 days ahead and chilled.

Angel-Hair Pasta with Fresh Tomato Sauce

Serves **4 to 6** | Active time: **20 minutes** | Start to finish: **25 minutes**

This dish showcases the simple perfection of beautifully ripe tomatoes: Some are chopped and some are grated (but none are cooked) to create a fresh, multi-textured sauce that is the essence of summer.

1 small garlic clove
Salt
3 pounds tomatoes
2 tablespoons fresh lemon juice
1 teaspoon sugar (optional)
½ teaspoon black pepper
1 pound dried capellini (angel-hair pasta)
½ cup chopped fresh basil

ACCOMPANIMENTS
Grated Parmigiano-Reggiano; extra-virgin olive oil for drizzling (optional)

▶ Mince garlic and mash to a paste with a pinch of salt using a large heavy knife.

▶ Core and coarsely chop two thirds of tomatoes. Halve remaining tomatoes crosswise, then rub cut sides of tomatoes against large holes of a box grater set in a large bowl, reserving pulp and discarding skin. Toss pulp with chopped tomatoes, garlic paste, lemon juice, 1 teaspoon salt, sugar (if using), and pepper. Let stand until ready to use, at least 10 minutes.

▶ While tomatoes stand, cook pasta in a 6- to 8-quart pot of boiling salted water, uncovered, until al dente, about 2 minutes. Drain in a colander and immediately add to tomato mixture, tossing to combine. Sprinkle with basil and serve with accompaniments.

COOKS' NOTE: The tomato mixture can stand at room temperature for up to 2 hours.

KITCHEN TIP
THERE'S NOTHING DELICATE ABOUT ANGEL HAIR

Angel-hair pasta, or capellini, sounds so ethereal that it's hard to believe it's actually more filling than many thicker pastas—spaghetti, say, or even rigatoni. We cooked and weighed equal amounts of several brands of capellini and spaghetti and discovered that in each case the capellini was heavier. Food scientist Shirley Corriher told us why: Capellini has a greater surface area than spaghetti and therefore more starch granules at the surface (the ones that absorb water most readily). So if you know you're feeding a crowd, substitute capellini for spaghetti for extra insurance that there'll be enough to go around.

Pasta with Spicy Anchovy Sauce and Dill Bread Crumbs

Serves **6** | Active time: **45 minutes** | Start to finish: **45 minutes**

Anchovy lovers will swoon over the sweetness of the onions, the saltiness of the fish, and the tactile pleasure of the crunchy bread crumbs. Hearty bucatini stands up to the robust flavors.

¾   cup extra-virgin olive oil
2   cups fresh bread crumbs (preferably from a baguette)
¼   cup chopped fresh dill
    Salt
¼   teaspoon black pepper
1   pound red onions, thinly sliced (3 cups)
1   (2-ounce) can flat anchovy fillets, drained and chopped
1   pound bucatini or perciatelli pasta (long tubular strands)
½   teaspoon hot red-pepper flakes

▶ Heat ¼ cup oil in a 12-inch heavy skillet over medium heat until it shimmers, then cook bread crumbs, stirring constantly, until deep golden and crisp, 6 to 8 minutes.

▶ Transfer bread crumbs to a bowl and toss with dill and ¼ teaspoon each of salt and black pepper.

▶ Wipe out skillet, then cook onions with ¼ teaspoon salt in remaining ½ cup oil over medium heat, stirring frequently, until very soft, 12 to 15 minutes. Add anchovies and cook, mashing anchovies into onions, until dissolved.

▶ Meanwhile, cook bucatini in a 6- to 8-quart pot of well-salted boiling water until al dente. Reserve ½ cup cooking water, then drain pasta.

▶ Stir red-pepper flakes and reserved water into anchovy sauce, then add pasta and toss to combine. Add about half of bread crumbs and toss to coat. Serve sprinkled with remaining bread crumbs.

Rigatoni with Marinara Sauce and Ricotta

Adapted from Michele Scicolone

Serves 4 | Active time: 40 minutes | Start to finish: 40 minutes

Pasta, lush tomatoes, and a pool of ricotta lend this dish all the flavor of a lasagne—without the heaviness. We serve the ricotta on the side for a more attractive presentation, but you can also stir it into the cooked pasta. The sauce tastes best when made with fresh tomatoes (which need to be peeled), but if you're short on time, canned work fine.

- 3 **pounds fresh plum tomatoes or 1 (28-ounce) can whole tomatoes in juice**
- 2 **large garlic cloves, crushed with side of a large heavy knife**
  Pinch of hot red-pepper flakes
- ¼ **cup olive oil**
  Salt
- 4 **fresh basil leaves, torn into bits**
- 1 **pound rigatoni**
- 1 **cup ricotta (½ pound; preferably fresh)**

ACCOMPANIMENT
  Grated Pecorino Romano

▸ If using fresh tomatoes, cut a shallow X in bottom of each with a paring knife and blanch tomatoes in 3 batches in a 5- to 6-quart pot of boiling water, 1 minute per batch.

▸ Transfer blanched tomatoes with a slotted spoon to a cutting board and, when cool enough to handle, peel, beginning from scored end, with knife, then halve lengthwise and seed. Chop tomatoes (fresh or canned), reserving juice (from cutting board or can).

▸ Cook garlic and red-pepper flakes in oil in a 4-quart heavy pot over moderate heat, stirring, until garlic is golden, about 5 minutes. Discard garlic, then add tomatoes with their juice and 1¼ teaspoons salt and simmer, uncovered, until sauce is thickened, about 20 minutes. Remove from heat and stir in basil and salt to taste.

▸ Cook pasta in a 6- to 8-quart pot of well-salted boiling water, uncovered, until al dente, then drain in a colander.

▸ Toss pasta with warm marinara sauce in a large bowl. Serve with ricotta and grated Pecorino Romano.

COOKS' NOTES: Sauce can be made ahead and cooled completely, uncovered, then chilled, covered, for up to 5 days or frozen in an airtight container for 2 months.

If using canned tomatoes, whose sodium content varies, use only ¼ teaspoon salt, then season your finished sauce with additional salt if desired.

KITCHEN TIP
MAKE YOUR OWN RICOTTA IN MINUTES

Homemade fresh ricotta is more delicate in flavor than any store-bought version and takes just a few minutes of active time. This recipe yields about 2 cups, enough for Rigatoni with Marinara Sauce. Topped with honey and cinnamon, it's great for dessert. Line a large sieve with a layer of heavy-duty (fine-mesh) cheesecloth and place it over a large bowl. Slowly bring 2 quarts whole milk, 1 cup heavy cream, and ¼ teaspoon salt to a rolling boil in a 6-quart heavy pot over moderate heat, stirring occasionally to prevent scorching. Add 3 tablespoons fresh lemon juice, then reduce heat to low and simmer, stirring constantly, until the mixture curdles, about 2 minutes. Pour the mixture into the lined sieve and let it drain for 1 hour. After discarding the liquid, chill the ricotta, covered; it will keep in the refrigerator for 2 days.

Capellini with Salmon and Lemon-Dill-Vodka Sauce

Serves **4** | Active time: **20 minutes** | Start to finish: **30 minutes**

The next time you cook salmon, make extra so you can serve this delicious pasta the following night. We are fond of the clean flavors in the Broiled Salmon with Citrus Yogurt Sauce on page 104, but any mildly seasoned salmon will work.

- 1 **medium onion, finely chopped**
- **Salt**
- 1 **tablespoon olive oil**
- 1 **cup reduced-sodium chicken broth**
- 1 **cup heavy cream**
- ½ **cup vodka**
- ½ **cup chopped fresh dill**
- 1½ **teaspoon grated fresh lemon zest**
- 2 **tablespoons fresh lemon juice**
- ¼ **teaspoon coarsely ground black pepper**
- 2 **cups flaked broiled salmon**
- 10 **ounces capellini (angel-hair pasta; about ⅔ of a 1-pound box)**

▶ Cook onion with salt in oil in a 3-quart heavy saucepan over moderate heat, stirring occasionally, until softened (but not browned), 5 to 6 minutes. Add broth, cream, vodka, and salt to taste and boil over moderately high heat, stirring frequently and reducing heat, if necessary, to keep liquid from foaming up too high and boiling over, until sauce is reduced to 2 cups, 10 to 12 minutes.

▶ Remove from heat and stir in dill, lemon zest and juice, and pepper. Reserve ½ cup sauce, then add salmon to saucepan and cook over moderately low heat until fish is just heated through, 2 to 3 minutes.

▶ While fish is heating, cook pasta in a 6- to 8-quart pot of well-salted boiling water until al dente. Reserve ½ cup cooking water, then drain pasta in a colander. Return pasta to pot, then toss with reserved sauce and cooking water.

▶ Serve pasta immediately, with fish and sauce spooned over the top.

Fettuccine with Sausage and Kale

Serves 4 to 6 | **Active time: 30 minutes** | **Start to finish: 30 minutes**

We've all heard the refrain about eating more dark, leafy greens. Here, nutritious-but-delicious kale teams up with spicy hot Italian sausage, ribbons of pasta, and a generous handful of Pecorino Romano. Mmm, just what the doctor ordered.

- 3 tablespoons olive oil
- 1 pound hot turkey or pork sausage, casings discarded and sausage crumbled
- ½ pound kale, tough stems and center ribs discarded and leaves coarsely chopped
- ½ pound dried egg fettuccine
- ⅔ cup reduced-sodium chicken broth
- ½ cup grated Pecorino Romano, plus additional for serving

▶ Heat oil in a 12-inch heavy skillet over moderately high heat until it shimmers, then cook sausage, breaking up any lumps with a spoon, until browned, 5 to 7 minutes.

▶ Meanwhile, blanch kale in a 6- to 8-quart pot of well-salted boiling water, uncovered, for 5 minutes. Remove kale with a large sieve and drain. Return cooking water in pot to a boil, then cook pasta in boiling water, uncovered, until al dente.

▶ Reserve 1 cup cooking water, then drain pasta in a colander.

▶ While pasta cooks, add kale to sausage in skillet and sauté, stirring frequently, until just tender, about 5 minutes. Add broth, stirring and scraping up any brown bits from bottom of skillet, then add pasta and ½ cup reserved cooking water to skillet, tossing until combined. Stir in cheese and thin with additional cooking water if desired.

▶ Serve immediately, with additional cheese on the side.

Cheesy Chicken and Mushroom Lasagne

Serves 4 | **Active time: 35 minutes** | Start to finish: **1½ hours**

No-boil lasagne noodles and rotisserie chicken are lifesavers: They can turn what's often perceived as a party dish into a practical weeknight supper. Unused lasagne noodles are handy for crumbling into soup.

1 **(10-ounce) package cremini or white mushrooms, thinly sliced**
3 **garlic cloves, minced**
  Salt and black pepper
1 **tablespoon olive oil**
5 **tablespoons unsalted butter**
½ **cup dry white wine**
½ **roast or rotisserie chicken, skin discarded, meat shredded (about 2¼ cups)**
3½ **cups whole milk**
¼ **cup all-purpose flour**
2 **teaspoons fresh thyme leaves**
¾ **cup grated Parmigiano-Reggiano**
12 **no-boil egg lasagne noodles (less than a 9-ounce package)**
1½ **cups coarsely grated Gruyère**

▶ Preheat oven to 425°F, with rack in middle.

▶ Cook mushrooms, garlic, ¼ teaspoon salt, and ⅛ teaspoon pepper in oil and 1 tablespoon butter in a 4-quart heavy saucepan over medium heat, stirring occasionally, until mushrooms are softened, about 3 minutes. Add wine and simmer briskly for 2 minutes. Transfer mushroom mixture to a large bowl and stir in chicken.

▶ Bring milk to a bare simmer in a medium saucepan. Melt remaining 4 tablespoons butter in 4-quart saucepan over medium-low heat. Add flour and cook roux, whisking constantly, for 3 minutes. Add hot milk in a fast stream, whisking constantly. Add thyme, ¾ teaspoon salt, and ½ teaspoon pepper and simmer, whisking occasionally, until thickened, 5 to 6 minutes. Remove from heat and reserve 1 cup sauce. Stir Parmesan into remaining sauce in pan, then stir into mushroom filling.

▶ Spread half of reserved plain sauce in 8-inch square baking pan to coat bottom. Add 3 lasagne sheets, overlapping slightly, and ⅓ of mushroom filling, spreading evenly, then sprinkle one quarter of Gruyère over top. Repeat 2 times. Top with remaining 3 lasagne sheets and remaining plain sauce, spreading evenly. Sprinkle with remaining Gruyère.

▶ Cover with foil, tenting to prevent foil from touching top of lasagne but sealing all around edge, and bake for 30 minutes. Remove foil and bake until cheese is golden, about 15 minutes more. Let lasagne stand for 10 minutes before serving.

Risotto with Asparagus and Morel Ragout

Serves 4 | **Active time: 35 minutes** | **Start to finish: 1½ hours**

Because the vegetables are cooked separately from the rice and then spooned over it in a rich ragout, this dish has a livelier, fresher taste than traditional risotto.

- ¾ **ounce dried morel mushrooms (1 cup) or ¼ pound fresh**
- 6½ **cups reduced-sodium chicken broth**
- 2 **cups water**
- 1 **pound medium asparagus, trimmed and cut diagonally into 1-inch pieces**
- ½ **small onion, finely chopped**
- 2 **tablespoons olive oil**
- 2 **cups Arborio rice (about 13 ounces)**
- ½ **cup dry white wine**
- ⅔ **cup grated Parmigiano-Reggiano**
- ½ **teaspoon salt**
- ½ **teaspoon black pepper**
- 4 **tablespoons (½ stick) unsalted butter, cut into tablespoons**
- 1 **teaspoon finely chopped garlic**
- ½ **cup frozen baby peas**
- 1 **teaspoon grated fresh lemon zest**
- 2 **teaspoons chopped fresh chives**

▶ If using dried morels, soak in warm water to cover for 30 minutes. Agitate dried morels in soaking water or fresh morels in cold water to dislodge grit, then lift from water, squeezing out excess liquid, and pat dry. Cut morels crosswise into ¼-inch slices.

▶ Bring broth and water to a boil in a 4-quart pot. Add asparagus and cook, uncovered, until crisp-tender, 3 to 4 minutes. Transfer asparagus with a slotted spoon to an ice bath, then drain and pat dry. Reserve 1 cup broth for ragout and keep remaining broth at a bare simmer.

▶ Cook onion in oil in a 5- to 6-quart heavy pot over moderate heat, stirring, until softened, about 3 minutes. Add rice and cook, stirring, for 1 minute. Add wine and simmer briskly, stirring constantly, until absorbed, about 1 minute. Add ½ cup hot broth mixture and simmer briskly, stirring, until broth is absorbed. Continue simmering and adding hot broth, about ½ cup at a time, stirring frequently and letting each addition be absorbed before adding the next, until rice is just tender and creamy-looking, 18 to 22 minutes. (Reserve leftover broth for thinning risotto.)

▶ Stir cheese, ¼ teaspoon salt, and ¼ teaspoon pepper into risotto, then let stand off heat, covered.

▶ Heat 2 tablespoons butter in a 10-inch heavy skillet over moderately high heat until foam subsides, then sauté morels and garlic, stirring occasionally, until garlic is pale golden. Add 1 cup reserved broth and bring to a boil. Stir in peas, asparagus, zest, and remaining ¼ teaspoon salt and ¼ teaspoon pepper and simmer, stirring occasionally, until vegetables are heated through, about 2 minutes. Remove from heat and swirl in remaining 2 tablespoons butter until incorporated.

▶ Thin risotto to desired consistency with some of leftover broth and divide among four shallow bowls. Spoon ragout on top and sprinkle with chives.

Bacon-and-Egg Rice

Serves 6 | Active time: **20 minutes** | Start to finish: **40 minutes**

This anytime Chinese meal mixes fried rice with onion, scallions, and the always welcome duo of bacon and eggs. We've used fresh rice in this recipe, but you could shave 25 minutes off the start-to-finish time by using leftover cooked rice (you'll need 6 cups).

2 cups long-grain white rice

2½ cups water

8 bacon slices, cut crosswise into ½-inch strips

6 large eggs

1½ teaspoons salt

½ teaspoon black pepper

1 medium onion, finely chopped

1 tablespoon vegetable oil

½ cup chopped scallions

1 teaspoon Asian sesame oil

▶ Bring rice and water to a boil in a 2½-quart heavy saucepan, then reduce heat to low and cook, tightly covered, until water is absorbed and rice is tender, about 20 minutes. Remove from heat and let stand, covered, for 5 minutes. Gently stir rice from top to bottom of saucepan with a heatproof rubber spatula.

▶ Cook bacon in a 12-inch nonstick skillet over moderate heat, stirring occasionally, until golden and crisp, about 6 minutes. Pour into a sieve set over a heatproof bowl and reserve bacon and fat separately.

▶ Whisk together eggs, ½ teaspoon salt, and ¼ teaspoon pepper in a medium bowl.

▶ Return 3 tablespoons fat to skillet and sauté onion over moderately high heat, stirring occasionally, until pale golden, about 5 minutes. Add eggs and cook, stirring, until eggs are just set, about 1 minute. Make a well in center of egg mixture, then pour in vegetable oil and 2 tablespoons reserved bacon fat. Add rice, remaining teaspoon salt, and remaining ¼ teaspoon pepper and cook, stirring, for 2 minutes. Add bacon, scallions, and sesame oil and cook mixture, stirring, for 1 minute. Serve immediately.

< *Greek Salad
with Orzo and
Black-Eyed Peas,
page 88*

CHAPTER 5

VEGETARIAN MAINS

It's not often you get the chance to do a lot of good without investing any extra time or effort. Eating vegetarian, even one night a week, is a one-stop-shopping way to do the right thing—for your health, your waist, your wallet; for the air, water, and soil as well. But we don't recommend eating vegetarian just because it's virtuous. Thank goodness it's easy and delicious, too. We love meatless meals because they showcase the ingredients—grains, vegetables, herbs, and spices—that lend character and nuance to any dish. Preparing vegetarian food forces us to pay closer attention to everything, from the smoky heat of chipotles in a quick pinto bean chili to the satisfying crunch of cucumber in a Greek orzo salad. It's the simplest way we know to become a better cook. And a happier eater.

Grilled Eggplant and Smoked-Gouda Bruschetta

Serves 4 | Active time: 45 minutes | Start to finish: 45 minutes

The components of these open-faced sandwiches are relatively straightforward, but the results are a revelation. And with gooey melted cheese, tender slabs of eggplant, and a tomato-parsley salsa, they're a wonderful main-course option for vegetarians and meat eaters alike.

KITCHEN TIP
HOW TO CHOOSE EGGPLANT

For this recipe, you want the freshest eggplant you can find. It should be firm, with smooth, taut skin and a nice sheen, and it should feel heavy in your hand; no blemishes or soft spots allowed. If you press it with your thumb, the skin should give slightly and then bounce right back. Also check the calyx, the fuzzy part around the stem; it should look fresh, not dried out.

- 1 **pound tomatoes, finely chopped (2½ cups)**
- ¼ **cup finely chopped fresh flat-leaf parsley**
- ½ **cup plus 2 tablespoons extra-virgin olive oil**
- 1 **tablespoon white-wine vinegar Black pepper**
- 1¼ **teaspoons salt**
- 1 **(8-ounce) piece smoked cheese, such as Gouda, mozzarella, or scamorza**
- 4 **(¾-inch-thick) slices country-style bread (from an 8-inch round loaf)**
- 2 **(1-pound) eggplants**

▶ Prepare grill for cooking over direct heat with medium-hot charcoal (moderate heat for gas); see "Grilling Procedure," page 11.

▶ While grill is heating, stir together tomatoes, parsley, 2 tablespoons oil, vinegar, ½ teaspoon pepper, and ¾ teaspoon salt.

▶ With a cheese plane or vegetable peeler, shave half of cheese into thin slices (if using mozzarella, thinly slice half of it with a knife) and cover with plastic wrap, reserving remainder for another use.

▶ Brush bread on both sides with 1 tablespoon oil per slice.

▶ Cut off top and bottom of each eggplant, then cut 2 (1-inch-thick) slices lengthwise from center of each eggplant, reserving remainder for another use.

Brush cut sides with 3 tablespoons oil (total) and sprinkle with remaining ½ teaspoon salt.

▶ Lightly oil grill rack, then grill eggplant slices (covered only if using a gas grill), loosening with a metal spatula and turning occasionally to avoid overbrowning, until very tender, 8 to 10 minutes. While eggplant is grilling, grill bread, turning over once, until grill marks form, 1 to 2 minutes total, and transfer to a platter. Top toast with salsa and drizzle evenly with remaining tablespoon oil.

▶ Transfer eggplant to a baking sheet, then top with sliced cheese. Return to grill and cook, covered for charcoal or gas, without turning, until cheese begins to melt, about 1 minute. Transfer each eggplant slice to a toast. Season with pepper to taste.

COOKS' NOTES: If you can't grill outdoors, you can cook the bread and eggplant in 2 batches on a lightly oiled two-burner ridged grill pan over moderate heat. Grill the eggplant, turning occasionally, for 10 to 13 minutes, then top with the cheese. Transfer eggplant to a large baking sheet and broil about 3 inches from preheated broiler until the cheese is just melted, about 1 minute.

The tomato mixture can be made 30 minutes ahead and kept at room temperature.

Summer Rolls with Sweet-and-Savory Dipping Sauce

Makes **8 rolls** | Active time: **45 minutes** | Start to finish: **45 minutes**

Vietnamese-style rolls are a great warm-weather dish: They require very little cooking. Thanks to bean thread noodles and baked tofu, they make a substantial meal, but pickled vegetables and a trio of herbs keep each sauce-dipped bite light and cool.

2   ounces dried bean thread noodles
1   small carrot, cut into thin matchsticks
1   Kirby cucumber, halved lengthwise, seeded, and cut into thin matchsticks
1   small jalapeño chile, cut into thin matchsticks
¼   cup rice vinegar (not seasoned)
¼   teaspoon sugar
1   tablespoon plus ¾ teaspoon fresh lime juice
¼   teaspoon salt
16   rice-paper rounds (*galettes de riz*; about 8 inches in diameter), plus additional in case some tear
4   romaine leaves, each torn into 4 pieces
10   ounces packaged baked tofu, cut into 3- by ⅓-inch sticks
1   cup fresh bean sprouts
½   cup each torn fresh basil, mint, and cilantro leaves (1½ cups total)
⅓   cup hoisin sauce
2   tablespoons chunky peanut butter
2   tablespoons water

▸ Soak noodles in a bowl of boiling-hot water for 10 minutes.

▸ Meanwhile, blanch carrot in boiling water until softened, about 45 seconds. Drain. Rinse under cold water, then transfer to a small bowl with cucumber, jalapeño, vinegar, sugar, 1 tablespoon lime juice, and salt. Let stand for 5 minutes. Reserve 2 tablespoons liquid and drain pickled vegetables.

▸ Drain noodles and rinse under cold water, then drain again and pat dry. Toss with remaining ¾ teaspoon lime juice and snip with kitchen shears 5 or 6 times.

▸ Fill a shallow pan with warm water. Soak 2 rice-paper rounds until they begin to soften, about 30 seconds, then let excess water drip off and stack them on a work surface so that they overlap almost completely, leaving 1 inch on either side. Put 2 pieces of romaine on bottom third of stack. Top with ⅛ of noodles (about 2 tablespoons), tofu (4 sticks), bean sprouts (about 2 tablespoons), herbs (3 tablespoons), and pickled vegetables (3 tablespoons). Roll up tightly around filling, folding in sides. Make 7 more rolls.

▸ Stir together hoisin sauce, peanut butter, water, and reserved 2 tablespoons pickling liquid. Serve rolls with dipping sauce.

COOKS' NOTE: The rolls and sauce can be made 4 hours ahead and chilled, the rolls covered with damp paper towels and then plastic wrap.

Greek Salad with Orzo and Black-Eyed Peas

Serves 4 | **Active time: 30 minutes** | **Start to finish: 45 minutes**

This refreshing vegetarian combo—a black-eyed-pea salad with tomatoes; orzo tossed with olives, red onion, and cucumber; and salty crumbles of feta cheese—is layered together in glass jars for a portable, picturesque picnic lunch. Certainly beats flimsy paper plates.

- ¾ cup orzo
- 1 (15-ounce) can black-eyed peas, rinsed and drained
- 1 large tomato, diced
- 2 tablespoons chopped fresh flat-leaf parsley
- 2 tablespoons red-wine vinegar
- 2 tablespoons extra-virgin olive oil
- 1 teaspoon salt
- ½ teaspoon black pepper
- ½ seedless cucumber, halved lengthwise, cored, and diced (1 cup)
- ½ cup pitted Kalamata olives, slivered
- ⅓ cup thinly sliced red onion
- 1 teaspoon grated lemon zest
- 2 tablespoons fresh lemon juice
- 1 tablespoon finely chopped fresh oregano
- 2–3 cups coarsely chopped romaine
- ½ pound feta, crumbled (1 cup)
- 4–8 peperoncini

SPECIAL EQUIPMENT
- 4 (16-ounce) wide-mouth jars or containers with lids

ACCOMPANIMENT
Pita chips

▶ Cook orzo according to package instructions. Drain in a sieve and rinse under cold water until cool. Drain well.
▶ Toss black-eyed peas, tomato, and parsley with vinegar, 1 tablespoon oil, ½ teaspoon salt, and ¼ teaspoon pepper. Marinate, stirring occasionally, for 15 minutes.
▶ Meanwhile, toss together orzo, remaining tablespoon oil, cucumber, olives, onion, lemon zest and juice, oregano, remaining ½ teaspoon salt, and remaining ¼ teaspoon pepper in a large bowl.
▶ Divide black-eyed-pea mixture (with juices) among jars and layer orzo salad, romaine, and feta on top. Add 1 or 2 peperoncini to each jar.
▶ Serve with pita chips.

COOKS' NOTE: Assembled jars can be chilled for up to 8 hours. Serve at room temperature.

Rava Dosas with Potato-Chickpea Masala

Serves **4** | Active time: **40 minutes** | Start to finish: **1 hour**

Rava dosas—savory, crisp-edged crepes popular in South India—are typically made from semolina and rice flours. Stuff them with hearty vegetables cooked in a blend of spices, chile, garlic, and ginger.

FOR MASALA FILLING

- 1½ **pounds Yukon Gold potatoes**
- ⅓ **cup grated dried unsweetened coconut**
- 2 **teaspoons cumin seeds**
- 1 **(3-inch) jalapeño chile, coarsely chopped, including seeds**
- 1 **(2½-inch) piece peeled fresh ginger, coarsely chopped**
- 3 **garlic cloves, smashed**
- 1 **tablespoon curry powder**
- ½ **teaspoon ground cinnamon**
- ½ **teaspoon ground turmeric**
- ⅓ **cup vegetable oil**
- 1¾ **cups water**
- 1 **teaspoon salt**
- 1 **large onion, chopped (about 3 cups)**
- 1 **(15- to 19-ounce) can chickpeas, rinsed and drained**
- ½ **cup frozen peas (do not thaw)**
- ½ **cup chopped fresh cilantro**

FOR RAVA DOSAS

- ½ **cup semolina flour**
- ½ **cup rice flour**
- ½ **cup all-purpose flour**
- ½ **teaspoon cumin seeds**
- ½ **teaspoon salt**
- 2 **cups water**
  Vegetable oil for brushing

▶ **MAKE MASALA FILLING:** Peel potatoes and cut into 1½-inch pieces. Cover with cold water in a bowl.

▶ Toast coconut in a 12-inch heavy skillet over medium heat, stirring occasionally, until golden, about 3 minutes. Transfer to a small bowl and wipe out skillet. Toast

cumin seeds in skillet over medium heat, stirring until fragrant and a shade darker, about 30 seconds. Transfer to another small bowl. Reserve skillet.

▶ Puree jalapeño, ginger, and garlic in a blender with curry powder, cinnamon, turmeric, oil, ¼ cup water, and salt until smooth. Transfer puree to skillet and cook over medium-high heat, stirring, until thickened slightly, about 1 minute. Add onion and cook, stirring occasionally, until it begins to soften.

▶ Drain potatoes, then add to onion with cumin seeds and cook over medium heat, stirring occasionally, until potatoes are barely tender, about 10 minutes.

▶ Add chickpeas and remaining 1½ cups water, scraping up any brown bits, then briskly simmer, covered, until potatoes are tender, 16 to 20 minutes more. Add peas and cook, covered, until just tender, about 3 minutes. Remove from heat and stir in toasted coconut and cilantro.

▶ **MAKE DOSAS WHILE POTATOES COOK:** Whisk flours, cumin seeds, salt, and water in a bowl.

▶ Generously brush a 12-inch nonstick skillet with oil and heat at medium high until it shimmers. Pour ½ cup batter into skillet, swirling to coat bottom. Cook, undisturbed, until dosa is set and edges are golden, about 2 minutes. Flip using a rubber spatula and cook dosa until underside is golden in spots, about 1 minute more.

Transfer to a plate. Make more dosas. Stack and cover loosely with foil to keep warm.

▶ To serve, spoon filling into dosas.

COOKS' NOTE: The masala filling, without the coconut and cilantro, can be made 8 hours ahead and chilled. Reheat before stirring in the coconut and cilantro.

Inside-Out Eggplant Parmigiana Stack

Serves **4** | Active time: **40 minutes** | Start to finish: **1 hour**

Panfried patties made with eggs and bread crumbs are a great way to use leftover eggplant parmigiana ingredients. In fact, the patties are so delicious that we made them the crisp showstoppers in this reconstruction.

FOR TOMATO SAUCE

- 2 **tablespoons olive oil**
- 1 **small onion, finely chopped**
- 1 **garlic clove, minced**
- 1 **(14- to 15-ounce) can whole tomatoes in juice**
- ⅓ **cup water**
- ½ **teaspoon sugar**
- ¼ **teaspoon salt**
- 3 **tablespoons finely chopped fresh basil**

FOR EGGPLANT STACKS

- 2 **(1-pound) eggplants**
- 6 **tablespoons olive oil, plus additional for drizzling**
- ¾ **teaspoon plus ⅛ teaspoon salt**
- ¾ **cup plain dry bread crumbs**
- ½ **cup grated Parmigiano-Reggiano**
- ½ **cup finely chopped fresh flat-leaf parsley**
- 2 **garlic cloves, minced**
- ¼ **teaspoon black pepper**
- 6 **large eggs, lightly beaten**
- ½ **cup water**
- ¼ **teaspoon hot red-pepper flakes**
- ½ **pound arugula, coarsely chopped**
- 1 **cup packed fresh basil leaves, coarsely chopped**
- ½ **pound cold fresh mozzarella, ends trimmed and remainder cut into 4 (½-inch-thick) slices**

▶ **MAKE TOMATO SAUCE:** Heat oil in a heavy medium saucepan over medium heat until it shimmers, then cook onion and garlic, stirring occasionally, until softened, about 6 minutes.

▶ Meanwhile, blend tomatoes with juice in a blender until almost smooth. Add to onion mixture in saucepan with water, sugar, and salt and simmer, partially covered, stirring occasionally, until slightly thickened, about

10 minutes. Stir in basil and keep warm, covered.

▶ **BAKE EGGPLANT:** Preheat oven to 450°F, with rack in lowest position.

▶ Trim ends, then cut 12 (⅓-inch-thick) rounds from widest portion of eggplants. Brush both sides with 2 tablespoons oil and season with ½ teaspoon salt (total). Bake on an oiled baking sheet, turning once, until golden and tender, 20 to 30 minutes. Transfer to a plate and keep warm, covered. Leave oven on.

▶ **MAKE EGG PATTIES AND SAUTÉ ARUGULA:** Stir together bread crumbs, Parmesan, parsley, half of garlic, and ¼ teaspoon each of salt and pepper, then stir in eggs and water.

▶ Heat 3 tablespoons oil in a 12-inch heavy skillet over medium heat until it shimmers. Drop 4 rounded ⅓-cupfuls of egg mixture into skillet and cook, turning once, until patties are golden brown and puffed, about 5 minutes. Transfer to paper towels to drain.

▶ Add remaining tablespoon oil to skillet and cook remaining garlic with red-pepper flakes, stirring, until garlic is golden, about 30 seconds. Add arugula, basil, and remaining ⅛ teaspoon salt and stir until just wilted.

▶ **ASSEMBLE STACKS:** Arrange 4 egg patties about 3 inches apart on a baking sheet. Top each with 2 tablespoons tomato sauce, 1 slice mozzarella, 1 eggplant slice, 2 more tablespoons tomato sauce, another eggplant slice, arugula mixture, and remaining eggplant. Bake until cheese melts, 5 to 10 minutes. Drizzle with additional oil and serve with sauce.

COOKS' NOTE: The sauce can be made 2 days ahead and chilled. The eggplant can be roasted 1 day ahead and chilled. Bring to room temperature.

Pinto Bean Mole Chili

Serves **6** | Active time: **30 minutes** | Start to finish: **45 minutes**

With notes of cumin, cinnamon, and chocolate playing off the earthy heat of anchos and chipotles, this meatless chili combines the best parts of a mole sauce and a Cincinnati-style chili. Its rich body makes it a seriously satisfying dinner any night of the week.

KITCHEN TIP

ANCHO AND CHIPOTLE CHILES

The dried version of a poblano, the heart-shaped ancho chile is slightly sweet and moderately hot. A smoke-dried jalapeño, the chipotle chile has definite heat and a distinctive smoky flavor. If you can't find dried chipotle, you can substitute a canned chile in adobo, a tomato-based sauce with spices.

2 dried ancho chiles, wiped clean
1 dried chipotle chile, wiped clean
1 teaspoon cumin seeds, toasted
1 teaspoon dried oregano, crumbled
⅛ teaspoon ground cinnamon, rounded
   Salt
2 medium onions, chopped
2 tablespoons olive oil
4 garlic cloves, finely chopped
3 medium zucchini or yellow squash, cut into ½-inch pieces
¾ pound kale, stems and center ribs discarded and leaves chopped
1 teaspoon grated orange zest
⅛ teaspoon sugar
1 ounce unsweetened chocolate, finely chopped
1 (14- to 15-ounce) can whole tomatoes in juice, drained, reserving juice, and chopped
1¼ cups water
3 (15-ounce) cans pinto beans, rinsed and drained

SPECIAL EQUIPMENT
   Electric coffee/spice grinder

ACCOMPANIMENTS
   Rice; chopped fresh cilantro; chopped scallions; sour cream

▶ Slit chiles lengthwise, then discard stems, seeds, and ribs. Heat a dry heavy skillet (not nonstick) over medium heat until hot, then toast chiles, opened flat, turning and pressing with tongs, until pliable and slightly changed in color, about 30 seconds. Tear into small pieces.

▶ Finely grind cumin seeds and chiles in grinder and combine with oregano, cinnamon, and 1½ teaspoons salt.

▶ Cook onions in oil in a large heavy pot over medium-high heat, stirring occasionally, until softened. Add garlic and cook, stirring, for 1 minute, then add chile mixture and cook, stirring, for 30 seconds. Stir in zucchini and kale and cook, covered, for 5 minutes. Add zest, sugar, chocolate, tomatoes with juice, and water and simmer, covered, stirring occasionally, until vegetables are tender, about 15 minutes.

▶ Stir in beans and simmer for 5 minutes. Season with salt and serve with accompaniments.

COOKS' NOTE: The chili improves in flavor if made 1 to 2 days ahead and chilled.

Huevos Rancheros

Serves 4 | **Active time: 30 minutes** | **Start to finish: 30 minutes**

Using chipotle chiles in adobo in this lively egg dish adds a subtle smoky flavor without the hassle of roasting and peeling fresh chiles. Plus, the recipe includes a nifty method for softening tortillas.

- 6 **tablespoons vegetable oil**
- 8 **(6-inch) corn tortillas**
- 2 **(14- to 15-ounce) cans whole tomatoes in juice**
- ½ **cup chopped white onion**
- ¼ **cup chopped fresh cilantro, plus additional for sprinkling**
- 1 **tablespoon chopped canned chipotle chiles in adobo**
- 2 **garlic cloves, coarsely chopped Salt**
- 8 **large eggs Black pepper**

▶ Preheat oven to 200°F, with rack in middle. Stack four ovenproof plates on oven rack to warm.

▶ Heat 1 tablespoon oil in a 10-inch heavy skillet over moderate heat until it shimmers. Stack 2 tortillas in skillet and cook for 30 seconds, then flip stack over with tongs and cook for 30 seconds more. While second tortilla cooks on bottom, turn top tortilla with tongs, keeping tortillas stacked. Flip stack again and cook in same manner, turning over top tortilla and flipping stack again so both tortillas are softened and both sides puff slightly then deflate (do not let them become browned or crisp). Wrap tortillas loosely in foil and keep warm in oven. Fry remaining tortillas in same manner, adding 1 tablespoon oil to skillet for each batch. (Do not clean skillet.)

▶ Puree tomatoes with their juice, onion, cilantro, chipotle, garlic, and salt to taste in a blender until very smooth. Carefully add mixture to hot skillet (it may spatter) and simmer, stirring occasionally, until salsa is slightly thickened, about 10 minutes.

▶ Heat 1 tablespoon oil in a 12-inch heavy nonstick skillet over moderately high heat until it shimmers, then crack 4 eggs into skillet and cook for 3 to 4 minutes for runny yolks, or to desired doneness. Transfer to a plate and keep warm, covered, then cook next 4 eggs in remaining tablespoon oil. Season eggs with salt and pepper.

▶ Spoon ¼ cup salsa onto each plate and top with 2 tortillas, slightly overlapping them. Top with eggs, remaining salsa, and cilantro.

COOKS' NOTE: The egg yolks in this recipe will not be fully cooked.

< Fish Fillets with Olives and Oregano, page 106

CHAPTER 6

SEAFOOD

Seafood is a curious thing. One of its greatest assets—that it takes mere minutes to prepare—disquiets certain cooks, as if anything so easy must be too good to be true. Nonsense, we say, accept this gift for what it is, and approach fish and shellfish with a light, deft hand. If you simply can't hold back (and let's be honest, sometimes we all get overzealous in the kitchen), direct your efforts to an easy salsa, sauce, or marinade; try making a creamy polenta on which to lay those pancetta-swaddled shrimp, or a simple beurre blanc to drizzle over your scallops. But go easy on the seafood—it will thank you with a kiss of sweet, briny flavor.

Salmon Cakes with Zucchini Fennel Slaw

Serves 2 | Active time: **25 minutes** | Start to finish: **25 minutes**

Salmon's moist, meaty texture makes it ideal for forming into cakes. Grated zucchini does double duty, bulking up the panfried patties and joining crisp fennel in a sprightly slaw.

¼ cup plus 2 tablespoons mayonnaise

4 teaspoons fresh lemon juice

⅓ cup chopped fresh chives

2 teaspoons grainy or Dijon mustard

¼ teaspoon cayenne

Salt and black pepper

2 medium zucchini, coarsely grated (3 cups)

½ pound skinless salmon fillet, chopped

12 Ritz or saltine crackers, crushed

½ medium fennel bulb, trimmed and thinly sliced

2 tablespoons olive oil

▶ Whisk together mayonnaise, 2 teaspoons lemon juice, chives, mustard, cayenne, and ½ teaspoon each salt and pepper in a medium bowl.

▶ Wrap 1½ cups zucchini in a kitchen towel and firmly squeeze out excess liquid. Transfer to a bowl and add salmon, crackers, and half of mayonnaise mixture, stirring to combine well.

▶ Add fennel and remaining zucchini and lemon juice to remaining mayonnaise mixture in medium bowl and toss to combine slaw. Season with salt and pepper.

▶ Form salmon mixture into 4 (3-inch) patties. Heat oil in a 9- to 10-inch nonstick skillet over medium heat until hot, then cook salmon cakes, carefully turning once, until golden and salmon is just cooked through, about 6 minutes total. Serve with slaw.

Broiled Salmon with Citrus Yogurt Sauce

Serves **4 to 6** | Active time: **20 minutes** | Start to finish: **35 minutes**

In a complicated world, there is comfort in simplicity: this subtly seasoned broiled salmon, for example, served with a creamy lime sauce. Leftovers are perfect in the Capellini with Salmon and Lemon-Dill-Vodka Sauce (page 72).

FOR SALMON
- Olive oil
- 1 (3-pound) piece salmon fillet with skin (1 inch thick at thickest part; preferably center cut)
- ⅜ teaspoon salt
- ¼ teaspoon black pepper

FOR SAUCE
- 1 cup plain whole-milk Greek yogurt or 1½ cups plain whole-milk yogurt (see Cooks' Notes)
- 2 tablespoons extra-virgin olive oil
- 1 tablespoon water, if desired
- 1¼ teaspoons grated fresh lime zest
- 1 tablespoon fresh lime juice
- 1 teaspoon grated fresh orange zest
- 2 teaspoons fresh orange juice
- ½ teaspoon salt
- ¼–½ teaspoon mild honey (to taste)

SPECIAL EQUIPMENT
- Pliers (preferably needlenose)

ACCOMPANIMENT
- Lime wedges

▶ Preheat broiler. Line rack of broiler pan with foil and lightly oil foil.

▶ Pat fish dry and check for bones by running your hand over fish from thinnest to thickest end. Remove any bones with pliers. Sprinkle fish with salt and pepper, then broil 4 inches from heat for 7 minutes. Cover fish loosely with foil and continue broiling until just cooked through, 7 to 9 minutes more.

▶ While salmon broils, whisk together all sauce ingredients in a bowl until combined.

▶ Serve salmon with sauce and lime wedges.

COOKS' NOTES: If reserving some salmon to make the capellini on page 72, set aside one third of the cooked fillet and separate into large (about 1½-inch) flakes, discarding skin and any dark flesh. (You should have about 2 cups.) Cool to room temperature, then chill, covered with plastic wrap, for up to 2 days.

If you can't find Greek yogurt, buy regular plain whole-milk yogurt and drain it in a sieve or colander lined with a double thickness of paper towels for 1 hour.

Fish Fillets with Olives and Oregano

Serves 4 | **Active time: 15 minutes** | **Start to finish: 30 minutes**

Elegant but easy, this fast fish dinner is simple enough to prepare on a weeknight and special enough to serve to company.

KITCHEN TIP
PITTING OLIVES

If you don't have an olive pitter, don't worry: All you need is a comfortably large knife. Line up a few olives on a cutting board and press them with the flat side of the knife. They'll split open, exposing the pits, which you can then slide right out. Green olives are less ripe and thus firmer than black olives, so you may have to cut them off the pit with a smaller knife.

4   (1¼-inch-thick) pieces white-fleshed skinless fish fillets, such as halibut (6 ounces each)
    Salt and black pepper
3   tablespoons extra-virgin olive oil
4   very thin lemon slices
½   cup dry white wine
⅓   cup pitted brine-cured green olives, such as picholine, halved lengthwise
1–1½   teaspoons fresh lemon juice
2   tablespoons finely chopped fresh oregano or ¾ teaspoons dried oregano, crumbled

SPECIAL EQUIPMENT
    2½-quart shallow ceramic or glass baking dish

▶ Preheat oven to 450°F, with rack in upper third.

▶ Pat fish dry and sprinkle with 1 teaspoon salt and ¼ teaspoon pepper. Heat 1 tablespoon oil in a 12-inch heavy skillet over moderately high heat until it shimmers, then sear fillets, skinned sides down, until browned well, 3 to 4 minutes. Transfer, seared sides up, to baking dish (reserve skillet), then top each fillet with a slice of lemon.

▶ Add wine to skillet and bring to a boil, scraping up any brown bits. Boil for 30 seconds, then pour around fish. Scatter olives around fish and bake, uncovered, until fish is just cooked through, 8 to 12 minutes.

▶ Transfer fish to a platter, then whisk lemon juice, oregano, and remaining 2 tablespoons oil into cooking liquid in baking dish. Season sauce with salt and pepper and spoon over fish.

Mussels in Lager

Serves 2 | Active time: **30 minutes** | Start to finish: **30 minutes**

Mussels are one of the great quick meals because they cook in less than 10 minutes. *Moules à la marinière*—mussels in white wine and garlic—may be their best-known preparation, but beer makes for an equally delicious broth. Soak up every last drop with crusty bread.

- 4 tablespoons (½ stick) unsalted butter
- 1 medium onion, chopped
- 2 celery ribs, cut into ¼-inch dice
- 1 cup drained canned diced tomatoes (from a 14- to 15-ounce can)
- 3 garlic cloves, finely chopped
- 1 teaspoon chopped fresh thyme
- 1 Turkish or ½ California bay leaf
- ½ teaspoon salt
- ¼ teaspoon black pepper
- 2 cups lager, such as Harp (16 ounces; pour beer slowly into measuring cup; do not measure foam)
- 2 pounds mussels (preferably cultivated), scrubbed well and beards removed
- 1 tablespoon Dijon mustard
- 2 tablespoons heavy cream
- ¼ cup chopped fresh flat-leaf parsley

ACCOMPANIMENT
- Crusty bread

▶ Heat butter in a wide 5- to 6-quart heavy pot over moderately high heat until foam subsides, then cook onion, celery, tomatoes, garlic, thyme, bay leaf, salt, and pepper, stirring occasionally, until vegetables are softened, about 4 minutes.

▶ Add beer and bring just to a boil. Add mussels and cook, covered, stirring occasionally, until mussels open wide, 4 to 6 minutes, transferring them to a bowl as they open. (Discard any mussels that remain unopened after 6 minutes.) Remove pot from heat.

▶ Stir together mustard and cream in a small bowl, then add mixture along with parsley to hot broth and whisk until combined. Discard bay leaf. Pour sauce over mussels and serve with crusty bread.

KITCHEN TIP

THE FRESHEST MUSSELS

Most of the mussels in the market today are cultivated; we prefer them not only because they're farmed in an environmentally responsible way but because they're so much cleaner, with fewer beards to scrub off. Remember, mussels are alive (or should be when you buy them), so freshness is key. If you can, ask for the harvest date and avoid any that are more than 4 days old. Another way to measure freshness is the sniff test—they should have the bright, deliciously briny smell of the sea. Give the mussels a quick rinse and drain when you get home, discard any cracked shells, then store them in a bowl covered with a wet towel. When it's time to cook them (which should be the same day you purchase them), tap any opened mussels on the counter. If they don't close their shells, discard them as well.

Shrimp and Pancetta on Polenta

Serves 4 | **Active time: 25 minutes** | Start to finish: **25 minutes**

Here, shrimp and pancetta join forces with creamy instant polenta in an Italian take on a Southern favorite, shrimp and grits.

½ **cup instant polenta**
Salt
¼ **pound pancetta, chopped**
2 **garlic cloves, minced**
¼ **teaspoon hot red-pepper flakes**
3 **tablespoons extra-virgin olive oil**
1 **(14-ounce) can diced tomatoes in juice**
1 **pound cleaned large shrimp**
Black pepper
1 **tablespoon chopped fresh flat-leaf parsley**

▶ Cook polenta according to package instructions in a heavy medium saucepan until thickened and creamy, about 5 minutes. Remove from heat and season with salt, then cover.

▶ Cook pancetta, garlic, and red-pepper flakes in 2 tablespoons oil in a 12-inch heavy skillet over medium heat, stirring, until garlic is pale golden, 2 to 3 minutes. Add tomatoes with their juice and simmer until liquid is reduced to about ¼ cup, 6 to 8 minutes. Add shrimp and cook, stirring occasionally, until shrimp are just cooked through, about 3 minutes. Season with salt.

▶ Spoon polenta into shallow bowls and top with shrimp mixture. Drizzle with remaining tablespoon oil, season with pepper, and sprinkle with parsley.

Indian Shrimp Curry

Serves 6 | **Active time: 45 minutes** | **Start to finish: 45 minutes**

If the sight of eight serrano chiles in a recipe sets off heat alarms in your brain, rest assured that this curry is not searingly hot, but nicely balanced by the natural sweetness of the shrimp and coconut. If you can find fresh curry leaves, great, but those who can't won't miss them.

- 6–8 serrano chiles (2 ounces total)
- 20 fresh curry leaves (optional)
- 5 garlic cloves, finely chopped
- 1 tablespoon finely chopped peeled fresh ginger
- 2 tablespoons vegetable oil
- 1 teaspoon whole mustard seeds
- 1 teaspoon ground coriander
- ½ teaspoon ground cumin
- ¼ teaspoon ground turmeric
- Salt and black pepper
- 1 medium onion, chopped
- 1 pound tomatoes, chopped
- 1 cup grated dried unsweetened coconut
- 2 pounds large shrimp in shell, peeled and deveined

ACCOMPANIMENT
- White rice

▶ Quarter chiles lengthwise (seed and devein if you want less heat). Cook chiles, curry leaves, garlic, and ginger in oil in a 12-inch heavy skillet over medium-high heat, stirring, until very fragrant and chiles are just softened, 1 to 2 minutes.

▶ Reduce heat to medium and add spices, 1 teaspoon salt, and ½ teaspoon pepper. Cook, stirring, until mustard seeds begin to pop, 1 to 2 minutes.

▶ Add onion and cook, stirring occasionally, until softened, about 4 minutes.

▶ Add tomatoes and coconut, then cook, covered, until tomatoes are softened, 4 to 6 minutes.

▶ Add shrimp and cook, uncovered, stirring, until just cooked through, 3 to 4 minutes. Season with salt and pepper. Serve with rice.

KITCHEN TIP
BUYING CURRY LEAVES

Spicy, citrusy curry leaves are used extensively in South Indian cooking. The leaves, often sold on the stem, can be found at Indian or Asian markets, where they might be labeled "*meetha neem*" or "*kari patta*." You can also find them online at www.ishopindian.com. Sealed in a plastic bag, they will last for about 2 weeks in the refrigerator or a month in the freezer. Avoid dried curry leaves; they are virtually tasteless.

Seared Scallops with Tarragon-Butter Sauce

Serves **4** | Active time: **20 minutes** | Start to finish: **20 minutes**

Beurre blanc—the classic French butter sauce—is a cinch to prepare and makes just about anything taste better. This take on it uses the scallops' juices to add complexity.

1¼ **pounds large sea scallops, tough ligament from side of each discarded**
Salt and black pepper
7 **tablespoons cold unsalted butter, cut into tablespoons**
2 **tablespoons finely chopped shallot**
¼ **cup dry white wine**
¼ **cup white-wine vinegar**
1 **tablespoon finely chopped fresh tarragon**

▶ Pat scallops dry and sprinkle with ¼ teaspoon each of salt and pepper (total).

▶ Heat 1 tablespoon butter in a 12-inch nonstick skillet over medium-high heat until foam subsides, then sear scallops, turning once, until golden brown and just cooked through, about 5 minutes total. Transfer to a platter.

▶ Add shallot, wine, and vinegar to skillet and boil, scraping up brown bits, until reduced to 2 tablespoons. Add juices from platter and if necessary boil until liquid is reduced to about ¼ cup. Reduce heat to low and add 3 tablespoons butter, stirring or whisking constantly until almost melted, then add remaining 3 tablespoons butter and swirl until incorporated and sauce is creamy. Stir in tarragon and salt to taste; pour sauce over scallops.

KITCHEN TIP
PREPPING SCALLOPS

Sea scallops cook quickly, but we do take the time to peel off the fibrous little bit on the side of the tender meat if it hasn't already been removed; it gets tough and chewy when cooked. Called the resilium, it's a hinge ligament that the bivalve uses to open and close its shell. Marine biologists use the ring pattern in the resilium to tell a scallop's age; each ring equals 1 year.

Boiled Lobster Dinner with Sesame Mayonnaise

Serves **4** | Active time: **10 minutes** | Start to finish: **30 minutes**

This one-pot meal—lobster, corn, and green beans—conjures up summer in New England. The simple sesame mayonnaise is outstanding for dunking and slathering.

¾–1 **pound trimmed green beans**

4 **ears shucked corn**

4 **(1¼- to 1½-pound) live lobsters**

⅔ **cup mayonnaise**

1 **teaspoon soy sauce**

1 **teaspoon Asian sesame oil**

▶ Cook green beans and corn in an 8-quart pot of salted boiling water until crisp-tender, about 4 minutes. Transfer to a platter and return water to a boil. Keep warm, loosely covered with foil.

▶ Plunge 2 lobsters headfirst into boiling water and cook, partially covered, over medium-high heat for 8 minutes (for 1¼-pound lobsters) to 9 minutes (for 1½-pound lobsters) from time they enter water. Transfer with tongs to a colander to drain. Return water to a boil and cook remaining lobsters.

▶ While lobsters cook, whisk together mayonnaise, soy sauce, and sesame oil.

▶ Serve lobsters with green beans, corn, and sesame mayonnaise.

< *Grilled*
Herbed
Poussins,
page 134

CHAPTER 7

CHICKEN

America loves chicken. In the past century, our consumption of poultry has gone up sevenfold. And little wonder: No other ingredient contributes so much to a meal for such minimal effort. In 10 minutes flat, chicken can add substance, flavor, and low-fat protein to your dinner lineup. And few other meats are as versatile. Chicken can crown the table as a holiday roast, but it's equally at home shredded in tostadas, braised with honey and lemon, lacquered in a sticky sesame sauce, or grilled in a fragrant herb paste. Even classics like meatballs or one-pot stews are these days as likely to be made with poultry as with beef. Clearly, this country has gone to the birds—and we're happy to be along for the ride.

Chicken Tostadas

Serves **6** | Active time: **45 minutes** | Start to finish: **45 minutes**

Once a way to make use of stale tortillas (by toasting and/or frying them), tostadas are so good that it wasn't long before people simply started using fresh tortillas. After biting into these crunchy, creamy, luscious layers of flavor, you'll see why.

KITCHEN TIP
MEXICAN CHEESES

Crema is a tangy cultured cream, similar to crème fraîche. In addition to providing flavor and texture, the cream helps soothe the heat of chiles. Cotija cheese, also known as *queso añejo*, is an aged cow's-milk cheese with a strong, salty presence.

1   **medium white onion**
1   **pound tomatoes, quartered**
2   **large garlic cloves**
1–2   **serrano chiles, stemmed**
½   **cup plus 2 tablespoons vegetable oil**
3   **cups shredded iceberg lettuce**
6   **large radishes, halved and sliced**
½   **cup chopped fresh cilantro**
    Salt
1   **rotisserie chicken, meat coarsely shredded (4 cups)**
6   **(6-inch) corn tortillas**
1   **(1-pound) can refried beans, heated**
1   **avocado, halved, pitted, and peeled**
½   **cup Mexican crema or sour cream**
¼   **cup crumbled cotija cheese or ricotta salata**

ACCOMPANIMENTS
    Sliced serrano chiles; lime wedges

▸ Preheat broiler.

▸ Cut half of onion into ¾-inch wedges, then chop remainder. Toss onion wedges, tomatoes, garlic, and whole chiles with 2 tablespoons oil on a rimmed baking sheet, spreading in 1 layer.

▸ Broil about 4 inches from heat until softened and charred, 10 to 15 minutes.

▸ Meanwhile, toss together lettuce, radishes, chopped onion, and half of cilantro.

▸ Puree roasted tomato mixture in a blender along with 1 or both roasted serranos (to taste) and 1 teaspoon salt until smooth (use caution when blending hot foods). Transfer puree to a bowl and stir in chicken, remaining cilantro, and salt to taste.

▸ Heat remaining ½ cup oil in a heavy medium skillet over medium-high heat until it shimmers. Fry tortillas, 1 at a time, turning once or twice and pressing with tongs to immerse, until golden brown, 45 to 60 seconds per tortilla. Drain briefly on paper towels, then transfer to plates.

▸ Spread tortillas thickly with heated refried beans, then top with chicken mixture. Slice avocado over tostadas and dollop with crema.

▸ Mound lettuce mixture on top and sprinkle with cheese. Serve with sliced chiles and lime wedges.

Sticky Sesame Chicken Wings

Serves **4** | Active time: **15 minutes** | Start to finish: **50 minutes**

Sweet, tangy, and spicy all at once, these sesame chicken wings (ideal for a picnic) require very little prep work—you just toss them in the sauce and roast.

1	**large garlic clove**
¾	**teaspoon salt**
2	**tablespoons soy sauce**
2	**tablespoons hoisin sauce**
2	**tablespoons mild honey**
1	**teaspoon Asian sesame oil**
	Pinch of cayenne
3	**pounds chicken wingettes or chicken wings (see Cooks' Note)**
1½	**tablespoons sesame seeds, lightly toasted**
1	**scallion (green part only), finely chopped**

▶ Preheat oven to 425°F, with rack in upper third. Line a large baking sheet (17 by 12 inches) with foil and lightly oil foil.

▶ Mince garlic and mash to a paste with salt using a large heavy knife. Transfer garlic paste to a large bowl and stir in soy sauce, hoisin, honey, sesame oil, and cayenne. Add wingettes to sauce, stirring to coat.

▶ Arrange wingettes in 1 layer on baking sheet and roast, turning over once, until cooked through, about 35 minutes. Transfer wingettes to a large serving bowl and toss with sesame seeds and scallion.

COOKS' NOTE: If using chicken wings instead of wingettes, cut off the tips from the chicken wings with kitchen shears or a large heavy knife and discard, then halve the wings at the joint.

Deviled Chicken Drumsticks

Serves **6** | Active time: **15 minutes** | Start to finish: **45 minutes**

Though they're quite irresistible right out of the oven, these juicy drumsticks (with a slight kick) are perfect picnic food, since they're also terrific cold or at room temperature.

12   chicken drumsticks (2½–3 pounds total)
½   cup Dijon mustard
¾   cup panko (Japanese bread crumbs)
¾   cup grated Parmigiano-Reggiano
¾   teaspoon cayenne
½   teaspoon salt
½   teaspoon black pepper
3   tablespoons unsalted butter, melted

▸ Preheat oven to 450°F, with rack in upper third.
▸ Pat chicken dry, then toss with mustard until evenly coated.
▸ Stir together panko, cheese, cayenne, salt, and pepper. Drizzle with butter and toss well.
▸ Dredge each drumstick in crumb mixture to coat, then arrange, without crowding, on a buttered large baking sheet. Roast until chicken is browned and cooked through, about 30 minutes. Serve warm or at room temperature.

COOKS' NOTE: The chicken can be roasted 1 day ahead and chilled.

KITCHEN TIP
THE SECRET TO CRISPNESS

For the crispiest coating, use panko—the Japanese bread crumbs that look more like shards of crunchy, airy bread than crushed crumbs (available in most supermarkets)—and mix with Parmesan and some melted butter before you coat the chicken. This helps distribute the butter evenly among the crumbs so that the mixture browns more evenly.

Sweet-and-Sour Chicken Thighs with Carrots

Serves 4 to 6 | **Active time: 30 minutes** | **Start to finish: 1 hour**

Expect crowds of would-be tasters at the stove when the intriguing aroma of these spice-rubbed chicken thighs—braised alongside carrots and onions in a sweet-and-sour honey-lemon sauce—fills the house.

- 8   small chicken thighs with skin and bone (2½–2¾ pounds total), trimmed
- 2   teaspoons salt
- 1¼   teaspoons paprika
- ¾   teaspoon ground cinnamon
- ½   teaspoon black pepper
- 1½   tablespoons olive oil
- 1   large onion, halved, then cut lengthwise into ¼-inch-wide strips
- 1   pound carrots, cut diagonally into 1-inch pieces
- 2   tablespoons minced garlic
- ½   cup water
- ¼   cup fresh lemon juice
- 2   tablespoons mild honey
- 1   tablespoon finely chopped fresh flat-leaf parsley
- 1   tablespoon finely chopped fresh cilantro

▶ Pat chicken dry. Stir together 1½ teaspoons salt with paprika, cinnamon, and pepper and rub onto chicken.

▶ Heat oil in a 12-inch heavy skillet over moderately high heat until it shimmers, then brown chicken in 2 batches, turning over once, about 10 minutes per batch. Transfer browned chicken to a plate.

▶ Discard all but 3 tablespoons fat from skillet, then add onion and carrots. Sprinkle with remaining ½ teaspoon salt and pepper to taste and cook over moderate heat, stirring occasionally, until onion is beginning to brown, 8 to 10 minutes. Add garlic and cook, stirring, for 1 minute.

▶ Return chicken, skin side up, to skillet, nestling it into vegetables. Stir together water, lemon juice, and honey until blended and add to skillet, then cook over moderately low heat, covered, until chicken is cooked through and carrots are tender, 25 to 30 minutes. Skim any fat from sauce, then add salt to taste. Sprinkle with herbs just before serving.

Grilled Chicken Breasts with Yogurt Sauce and Mint Salad

Serves 6 | Active time: 15 minutes | Start to finish: 35 minutes

The four Cs—chili powder, cumin, coriander, and cinnamon—are a spice combination that work magic on all kinds of meat and poultry. Here, they blend with yogurt in a quick marinade for chicken breasts in a dish that will transport you to the Mediterranean.

- 2¼ **cups plain yogurt (18 ounces; preferably whole-milk)**
- 3 **tablespoons olive oil**
- 2½ **tablespoons fresh lemon juice**
- **Salt**
- 1 **tablespoon chili powder**
- ¾ **teaspoons ground cumin**
- ¾ **teaspoons ground coriander**
- ¾ **teaspoons black pepper**
- ¼ **teaspoon ground cinnamon**
- 6 **skinless boneless chicken breast halves (2¼–2½ pounds total)**
- 1 **cup small fresh mint leaves**
- 2 **tablespoons minced shallot**

▶ Whisk together 1 cup yogurt, 2 tablespoons oil, 1 tablespoon lemon juice, 2 teaspoons salt, and spices, then add chicken and turn until coated well. Marinate at room temperature for 20 minutes.

▶ While chicken is marinating, prepare grill for cooking (see "Grilling Procedure," page 11). While grill is heating, whisk together remaining 1¼ cups yogurt, 1½ tablespoons lemon juice, and salt to taste.

▶ Grill chicken (discard marinade), covered only if using gas grill, on lightly oiled grill rack, turning over occasionally, until just cooked through, 10 to 12 minutes total. Transfer chicken to a platter.

▶ Toss together mint, shallot, and remaining tablespoon oil in a small bowl. Drizzle chicken with yogurt sauce and top with mint salad.

COOKS' NOTE: If you aren't able to grill outdoors, you can cook the chicken in a hot lightly oiled large ridged grill pan over medium heat.

Baked Chicken Meatballs with Peperonata

Serves 4 | Active time: 25 minutes | Start to finish: 45 minutes

These moist, flavorful meatballs speckled with pancetta and glazed with tomato paste are wonderful made with white or dark meat.

FOR PEPERONATA

- 3   red bell peppers, cut into strips
- 1½ tablespoons extra-virgin olive oil
- 1½ tablespoons drained capers
- 1   teaspoon red-wine vinegar
- ⅛ teaspoon hot red-pepper flakes

FOR MEATBALLS

- 3   slices Italian bread, torn into pieces (1 cup)
- ⅓ cup milk
- 3   ounces sliced pancetta, finely chopped
- 1   small onion, finely chopped
- 1   small garlic clove, minced
- 2   tablespoons extra-virgin olive oil
- ½ teaspoon salt
- ½ teaspoon black pepper
- 1   large egg
- 1   pound ground chicken
- 3   tablespoons finely chopped fresh flat-leaf parsley
- 1   tablespoon tomato paste

ACCOMPANIMENT

Garlic bread made from remainder of Italian loaf

▶ **MAKE PEPERONATA:** Preheat oven to 400°F, with racks in upper and lower thirds.

▶ Toss bell peppers with 1 tablespoon oil, then roast on a baking sheet in lower third of oven, stirring occasionally, until tender and browned, about 35 minutes.

▶ Stir together capers, vinegar, red-pepper flakes, and remaining ½ tablespoon oil in a medium bowl and set aside.

▶ **MAKE MEATBALLS WHILE PEPPERS ROAST:** Soak bread in milk in a small bowl until softened, about 4 minutes.

▶ Cook pancetta, onion, and garlic in 1 tablespoon oil with salt and pepper in a 10-inch skillet over medium heat until onion is softened, about 6 minutes. Cool slightly.

▶ Squeeze bread to remove excess milk, then discard milk. Lightly beat egg in a large bowl, then combine with chicken, pancetta mixture, bread, and parsley. Form 12 meatballs and arrange on another baking sheet.

▶ Stir together tomato paste and remaining tablespoon oil and brush over meatballs, then bake in upper third of oven until meatballs are just cooked through, 15 to 20 minutes.

▶ Toss bell peppers with caper mixture. Serve meatballs with peperonata and garlic bread.

Chicken in Riesling

Serves **4** | Active time: **30 minutes** | Start to finish: **1 hour**

Though *coq au vin* is perhaps the best-known incarnation of the French dish, most regions of France have versions made with local wines. Alsace's dry Riesling lends a gentle richness to this comforting meal that has all the depth of a slowly simmered stew but is ready in just an hour.

KITCHEN TIP
REMOVING THE BACKBONE

The easiest method is to put the chicken, breast side down, on a cutting board so that the backbone is facing up, running down the length of the chicken. Using poultry or sturdy kitchen shears, cut along both sides of the backbone to free it from the chicken. Don't throw it away, though. Freeze it and add it to the pot the next time you make chicken stock.

1 **whole chicken (about 3½ pounds), backbone discarded and chicken cut French style into 8 pieces (see Cooks' Note)**
Salt and black pepper
1 **tablespoon vegetable oil**
3 **tablespoons unsalted butter**
4 **medium leeks**
2 **tablespoons finely chopped shallot**
4 **medium carrots, halved diagonally**
1 **cup dry white wine (preferably Alsatian Riesling)**
1½ **pounds small (2-inch) red potatoes**
2 **tablespoons finely chopped fresh flat-leaf parsley**
½ **cup crème fraîche or heavy cream**
Fresh lemon juice

▶ Preheat oven to 350°F, with rack in middle.

▶ Pat chicken dry and sprinkle with 1 teaspoon salt and a rounded ¾ teaspoon pepper. Heat oil with 1 tablespoon butter in a wide 3½- to 5-quart heavy ovenproof pot over medium-high heat until foam subsides, then brown chicken in 2 batches, turning once, about 10 minutes total per batch. Transfer to a plate.

▶ Meanwhile, wash leeks and pat dry. Finely chop white and pale green parts only.

▶ Pour off fat from pot, then cook leeks, shallot, and ¼ teaspoon salt in remaining 2 tablespoons butter, covered, over medium-low heat, stirring occasionally, until leeks are pale golden, 5 to 7 minutes. Add chicken, skin side up, with any juices from plate, carrots, and wine and boil until liquid is reduced by half, 3 to 4 minutes. Cover pot and braise chicken in oven until cooked through, 20 to 25 minutes.

▶ While chicken braises, peel potatoes, then generously cover with cold water in a 2- to 3-quart saucepan and add 1½ teaspoons salt. Bring to a boil, then simmer until potatoes are just tender, about 15 minutes. Drain in a colander, then return to saucepan. Add parsley and shake to coat.

▶ Stir crème fraîche into chicken mixture and season with salt, pepper, and lemon juice to taste, then add potatoes.

COOKS' NOTE: A chicken cut French style yields 2 breast halves with wings attached, halved crosswise for a total of 4 breast pieces, 2 drumsticks, and 2 thighs. If you don't want to cut up a whole chicken, you can use 3 pounds of chicken parts.

Grilled Herbed Poussins

Serves 4 | Active time: **15 minutes** | Start to finish: **35 minutes**

An herb paste smeared onto these birds adds a concentrated taste of summer any time of year. Poussins or Cornish hens are ideal, since they're small enough to cook through before the herbs can threaten to burn.

¼   **cup chopped fresh basil**
1½ **tablespoons finely chopped fresh rosemary**
1   **tablespoon fresh thyme leaves**
2   **fresh bay leaves, finely chopped (optional)**
3   **tablespoons extra-virgin olive oil**
2   **small garlic cloves, chopped**
1   **tablespoon salt**
½   **teaspoon black pepper**
4   **poussins (1–1¼ pounds each) or small Cornish hens, backbones cut out and birds split in half**

▶ Blend together herbs, oil, garlic, salt, and pepper in a blender until finely chopped, then rub all over poussins.
▶ Prepare grill for indirect-heat cooking over medium-hot charcoal (medium-high heat for gas); see "Grilling Procedure," page 11.
▶ Oil grill rack, then grill poussins, skin sides down first, directly over coals, turning once, until well browned, 2 to 3 minutes. Move poussins to area with no coals underneath and grill, covered, until just cooked through, 15 to 20 minutes more. Transfer poussins to a platter and let stand for 10 minutes.

COOKS' NOTES: The poussins can be rubbed with herb paste 1 day ahead and chilled.

    To cook the poussins indoors, brown them as above in a hot large ridged grill pan over medium-high heat, then cover with an inverted roasting pan. Reduce the heat to medium and cook for about 18 minutes.

< *Korean-Style Grilled Flank Steak,* page 139

CHAPTER 8

BEEF, PORK & LAMB

Sure, we still know a handful of diehard meat-and-potatoes guys. But these days, we also know a lot of meat-and-tomato folks (of both genders), not to mention people who take their meat with gingerroot, Sriracha, or Mexican chiles. And thank heavens for that. The deep, savory character of red meat is offset by such a wide range of other ingredients that just playing with the options is delectable—to say nothing of eating them. Look for quick-cooking cuts—steaks, cutlets, chops; in a trice you can sear up a weeknight meal that's every bit as grand and stylish as an old-fashioned *Honey-I'm-home* supper (Scotch on the rocks optional).

Porterhouse Steak with Pan-Seared Cherry Tomatoes

Serves 4 | **Active time: 35 minutes** | **Start to finish: 45 minutes**

Delivering a lot of glamour for very little work, this gorgeous dish balances the rich flavor of the steak with the tomatoes' acidity. Take care not to overcook the tomatoes—they should be in the pan just long enough to release some of their juices, which create a natural sauce for the steak.

3 tablespoons olive oil
2 (1½-inch-thick) porterhouse steaks
   Kosher salt and black pepper
6 large garlic cloves, thinly sliced
2 pints mixed cherry tomatoes
6 large thyme sprigs
1½ cups coarsely torn fresh basil leaves

▶ Preheat oven to 375°F, with rack in middle.
▶ Heat 1 tablespoon oil in a 12-inch heavy skillet over medium-high heat until it shimmers.
▶ Pat steaks dry and sprinkle with 4 teaspoons salt and 1½ teaspoons pepper.
▶ Sear steaks 1 at a time, turning once, until well browned, about 10 minutes total per steak. Transfer steaks to a baking sheet (do not clean skillet) and cook in oven until an instant-read thermometer inserted in center registers 120°F for medium-rare, about 6 minutes. Let stand on a platter for 15 minutes.
▶ Pour off fat from skillet. Add remaining 2 tablespoons oil and heat over medium-high heat until it shimmers, then sauté garlic until golden. Transfer to a plate. Add tomatoes and thyme to hot oil and cook, covered, stirring occasionally, until tomatoes begin to wilt, about 2 minutes. Stir in any meat juices from platter and season with salt and pepper. Scatter basil on tomatoes and spoon over steaks.

Korean-Style Grilled Flank Steak

Serves 4 | **Active time: 25 minutes** | **Start to finish: 45 minutes**

Serving flank steak (a favorite for the grill) Korean style is always a hit—guests make lettuce-leaf bundles with rice and thin slices of meat and do the garnishing on their own.

¼ cup soy sauce
2 tablespoons rice vinegar (not seasoned)
1 tablespoon grated peeled fresh ginger
1 garlic clove, minced
2 teaspoons Sriracha (Southeast Asian chile sauce)
2 teaspoons sugar
1½ teaspoons Asian sesame oil
1–1¼ pounds flank steak
2 scallions, finely chopped
2 tablespoons sesame seeds, toasted

ACCOMPANIMENTS
White rice; soft leaf lettuce

▶ Stir together soy sauce, vinegar, ginger, garlic, Sriracha, sugar, and sesame oil.
▶ Prepare a gas grill for direct-heat cooking over medium-high heat; see "Grilling Procedure," page 11.
▶ Oil grill rack, then grill steak, covered, turning over once, 6 to 8 minutes for medium-rare.
▶ Transfer steak to a cutting board and drizzle with 2 tablespoons sauce, then let stand, uncovered, for 5 minutes. Thinly slice steak across the grain. Serve with remaining sauce, scallions, and sesame seeds, accompanied by rice and lettuce leaves.

Grilled Skirt Steaks with Tomatillos Two Ways

Serves **4 to 6** | Active time: **30 minutes** | Start to finish: **45 minutes**

Rich skirt steak begs for an assertive, acidic accompaniment. The tomatillo twofer showcases the fruit's different personalities. In the cooked salsa, its flavor is round and lemony; in the salad, fresh lime juice sharpens the tomatillos' raw brightness.

KITCHEN TIP

SKIRT STEAK 101

One of the most flavorful cuts of beef, skirt steak is long and flat, with a well-marbled diagonal grain and a deep red color. It's thin but uneven, so you may want to cut it into sections of uniform thickness so that they'll cook more evenly. Slice it against the grain when serving for maximum tenderness.

FOR TOMATILLO SALSA

- 4 **dried pasilla or guajillo chiles, wiped clean**
- 3–4 **teaspoons chopped canned chipotle chiles in adobo (to taste)**
- 1 **pound fresh tomatillos, husked and rinsed, then quartered**
- 1 **cup packed cilantro sprigs**
- 2 **garlic cloves**
- 1 **tablespoon packed dark brown sugar**
- 1 **teaspoon molasses (not blackstrap)**
- ½ **teaspoon ground cumin**
- 1 **teaspoon salt**
- ⅓ **cup vegetable oil**

FOR STEAKS AND TOMATILLO SALAD

- ¼ **cup vegetable oil**
- ¾ **teaspoons ground cumin**
  Salt and black pepper
- 1¾ **pounds skirt steak, halved**
- ½ **pound fresh tomatillos, husked and rinsed**
- 1 **cup fresh cilantro leaves**
- 2 **teaspoons finely chopped shallot**
- 2 **teaspoons fresh lime juice**

▶ **MAKE SALSA:** Slit dried chiles lengthwise, then remove stems, seeds, and ribs. Heat a dry heavy skillet (not nonstick) over medium heat until hot, then toast chiles, opened flat, turning and pressing with tongs, until more pliable and slightly changed in color, about 1 minute. Cover chiles with hot water in a bowl and soak until softened, about 20 minutes, then drain.

▶ Puree dried chiles, chipotles, tomatillos, cilantro, garlic, brown sugar, molasses, cumin, and salt in a blender until smooth, about 1 minute.

▶ Heat oil in a 10-inch heavy skillet over medium-high heat until it shimmers, then cook salsa (it will spatter), stirring occasionally, until thicker, 5 to 8 minutes.

▶ **GRILL STEAKS:** Prepare a grill for direct-heat cooking over hot charcoal (high heat for gas); see "Grilling Procedure," page 11.

▶ Whisk together 2 tablespoons oil, cumin, 1½ teaspoons salt, and 1 teaspoon pepper, then coat steaks.

▶ Oil rack, then grill steaks, covered only if using a gas grill, turning once, until grill marks appear, 4 to 6 minutes total for medium-rare. Let steaks rest on a cutting board, loosely covered with foil, for 10 minutes.

▶ **MAKE SALAD WHILE STEAKS REST:** Thinly slice tomatillos and toss with cilantro, shallot, lime juice, remaining 2 tablespoons oil, and salt and pepper to taste.

▶ Cut steaks into serving pieces and top with salsa and salad.

COOKS' NOTES: The steaks can be cooked in an oiled two-burner grill pan on medium-high, 4 to 10 minutes for medium-rare.

The salsa (not the salad) can be made 1 day ahead and chilled. Rewarm before serving.

Crisp Pork Medallions with Caper Sauce

Serves 4 | **Active time: 30 minutes** | **Start to finish: 35 minutes**

Bread-crumb-coated pork medallions are golden on the outside, moist on the inside. The caper-yogurt sauce provides a burst of briny flavor.

FOR SAUCE

⅔ cup plain whole-milk yogurt

3 tablespoons mayonnaise

2 tablespoons drained bottled capers, finely chopped

1 tablespoon finely chopped fresh flat-leaf parsley

⅛ teaspoon black pepper

FOR PORK

1½–1¾ pounds pork tenderloin

¾ cup all-purpose flour

1 teaspoon salt

¼ teaspoon black pepper

2 large eggs

1 cup fine dry bread crumbs

About 1 cup vegetable oil for panfrying

SPECIAL EQUIPMENT

Instant-read thermometer

ACCOMPANIMENTS

Lemon wedges; watercress or other baby greens

▶ **MAKE SAUCE:** Stir together all ingredients, then chill, covered, until ready to use.

▶ **COOK PORK:** Preheat oven to 350°F, with rack in middle.

▶ Cut pork crosswise into 1¼-inch-thick slices (medallions).

▶ Whisk together flour, salt, and pepper in a shallow bowl.

▶ Whisk eggs with a pinch of salt in another shallow bowl and put bread crumbs in a third shallow bowl.

▶ Working with 1 medallion at a time, dredge in flour, shaking off excess, and dip in egg, letting excess drip off, then coat with crumbs, pressing to help them adhere. Arrange pork in 1 layer on a baking sheet.

▶ Heat ¼ inch oil in a 12-inch heavy skillet over moderate heat until it shimmers, then panfry medallions, turning over once, until golden brown, 6 to 8 minutes total. Transfer to a clean baking sheet and roast in oven until thermometer inserted horizontally into center of meat registers 145°F to 150°F, 6 to 7 minutes.

▶ Serve pork with sauce, lemon wedges, and watercress.

COOKS' NOTE: The sauce can be made 1 day ahead and chilled.

Herb-Roasted Pork Loin

Serves 8 | **Active time: 20 minutes** | **Start to finish: 1½ hours**

The pork loin roasts on rosemary, thyme, sage, and savory sprigs that infuse the meat with flavor and mingle with the mustard and shallot coating. The luscious sauce is argument enough for keeping a bottle of dry vermouth on hand.

KITCHEN TIP

GOING WHOLE HOG

Although any supermarket pork roast will work beautifully here, for a special occasion you may want to splurge on a loin from one of the increasingly popular heritage breeds. Mass-market pork, bred to be extra-lean, has lost much of the fat that keeps meat juicy and flavorful. Berkshire pork, on the other hand, is known for its marbled flesh and rich flavor. It and other heritage breeds, particularly those that were pasture-raised, are worth seeking out (good sources are: heritagefoodsusa.com and flyingpigsfarm.com).

FOR PORK

- 1 (4- to 4½-pound) boneless pork loin roast, trimmed
- 1¾ teaspoons salt
- 1½ teaspoons black pepper
- 2 tablespoons plus 1 teaspoon olive oil
- 6 rosemary sprigs
- 8 large thyme sprigs
- 8 sage sprigs
- 8 savory sprigs (optional)
- ½ cup finely chopped shallots (4 to 5)
- 2 tablespoons finely chopped garlic
- 3 tablespoons Dijon mustard

FOR SAUCE

- ⅓ cup dry vermouth
- 2 teaspoons Dijon mustard
- 1¾ cups reduced-sodium chicken broth
- 1½ tablespoons unsalted butter
- 1½ tablespoons all-purpose flour

SPECIAL SQUIPMENT

Instant-read thermometer

▶ **ROAST PORK:** Preheat oven to 350°F, with rack in middle.

▶ Pat pork dry and season with salt and pepper. Straddle a flameproof roasting pan over two burners, then heat 1 tablespoon oil over medium-high heat until it shimmers. Brown pork on all sides, then transfer to a large plate.

▶ Put a metal rack in pan and arrange half of herbs down middle of rack. Stir together shallots, garlic, mustard, and

1 tablespoon oil and smear over top and sides of roast, then put roast, fat side up, on top of herbs. Roast for 1 hour. Toss remaining herbs with remaining teaspoon oil and arrange on top of roast.

▶ Continue roasting until an instant-read thermometer registers 140°F to 145°F, 5 to 15 minutes more (temperature will rise 5 to 10 degrees as it rests). Transfer pork to a cutting board and let rest for 15 to 25 minutes.

▶ **MAKE SAUCE WHILE PORK RESTS:** Remove rack from pan and discard herbs from rack. Straddle pan across two burners on medium heat. Add vermouth and mustard and deglaze by boiling, stirring and scraping up brown bits, until reduced by half. Add broth and simmer for 3 minutes. Strain through a fine-mesh sieve into a 2-cup measure. If you have more than 1½ cups, boil to reduce; if less, add water.

▶ Melt butter in a heavy medium saucepan over medium heat. Whisk in flour and cook, whisking, until pale golden, about 3 minutes. Whisk in vermouth mixture and simmer until slightly thickened, about 3 minutes.

▶ Serve pork with sauce.

Sausage and Lentils with Fennel

Serves 4 | **Active time: 35 minutes** | Start to finish: **45 minutes**

Sweet Italian sausage, tender fennel, and rustic French lentils come together in a full-bodied dish to warm a chilly night.

1 **cup dried lentils (preferably French green lentils; 7 ounces)**

4½ **cups cold water**
   Salt

1 **medium (¾-pound) fennel bulb, stalks discarded, reserving fronds**

3½ **tablespoons olive oil**

1 **medium onion, finely chopped**

1 **carrot, cut into ¼-inch dice**

½ **teaspoon fennel seeds**

1¼ **pounds sweet Italian sausage links**

3 **tablespoons chopped fresh flat-leaf parsley**

½ **teaspoon black pepper**

1 **tablespoon red-wine vinegar, or to taste**
   Extra-virgin olive oil for drizzling

▶ Bring lentils, water, and ½ teaspoon salt to a boil in a 2-quart heavy saucepan, then reduce heat and simmer, uncovered, until lentils are just tender but not falling apart, 12 to 25 minutes.

▶ While lentils simmer, cut fennel bulb into ¼-inch dice and chop enough fennel fronds to measure 2 tablespoons. Heat 3 tablespoons oil in a 3- to 4-quart heavy saucepan over moderate heat until it shimmers, then cook onion, carrot, fennel bulb, fennel seeds, and 1 teaspoon salt, covered, stirring occasionally, until vegetables are very tender, about 10 minutes.

▶ Meanwhile, lightly prick sausages in a couple of places with tip of a sharp knife, then cook in remaining ½ tablespoon oil in a 10-inch nonstick skillet over moderately high heat, turning occasionally, until golden brown and cooked through, 12 to 15 minutes. Transfer to a cutting board.

▶ Drain lentils in a sieve set over a bowl and reserve cooking water. Stir lentils into vegetables with enough cooking water to moisten (¼ to ½ cup) and cook over moderate heat until heated through. Stir in parsley, pepper, 1 tablespoon vinegar, and 1 tablespoon fennel fronds. Season with vinegar and salt.

▶ Cut sausages diagonally into ½-inch slices and serve on top of lentils with remaining fronds sprinkled over. Drizzle with extra-virgin olive oil.

Herbed Lamb, Tomato, and Zucchini Kebabs

Serves 4 | **Active time: 1 hour** | **Start to finish: 1¾ hours**

Kebabs are not only fun to eat, they also save time: It takes less than 10 minutes for these lamb cubes to cook up medium-rare. The marinade infuses both the meat and the vegetables with South of France flavor.

2–3   **large garlic cloves (to taste)**
      Salt
6   **tablespoons fresh lemon juice**
      Black pepper
1   **cup olive oil**
3   **tablespoons finely chopped fresh thyme**
2   **tablespoons finely chopped fresh rosemary**
1   **(2-pound) piece trimmed boneless leg of lamb, cut into 1¼-inch cubes**
3   **medium zucchini (1½ pounds total)**
24   **large cherry tomatoes (¾ pound)**
1   **tablespoon Dijon mustard**

SPECIAL EQUIPMENT
16   **(12-inch) wooden skewers, soaked in warm water for 1 hour**

▶ Mince garlic and mash to a paste with 1½ teaspoons salt using a large heavy knife.

▶ Whisk together garlic paste, lemon juice, and 1½ teaspoons pepper in a large bowl, then whisk in oil, thyme, and rosemary until combined well. Put lamb in a large sealable bag, then add ½ cup herb marinade and seal bag, pressing out excess air. Marinate lamb at room temperature for 1 hour.

▶ Meanwhile, halve zucchini lengthwise, then cut diagonally crosswise to create triangle shapes. Put zucchini in another large sealable bag, then pour ¼ cup of reserved marinade over zucchini and seal bag, pressing out excess air. Marinate zucchini at room temperature for 1 hour. (Marinating zucchini any longer will result in a mushy texture.)

▶ Prepare grill for cooking over direct heat with medium-hot charcoal (moderately high heat for gas); see "Grilling Procedure," page 11.

▶ While grill is heating, drain lamb, discarding marinade, then thread cubes ¼ inch apart onto 8 skewers. Drain zucchini, discarding marinade, then thread zucchini onto 4 skewers (without lamb). Thread tomatoes onto remaining 4 skewers.

▶ Puree remaining marinade with mustard in a blender until emulsified and transfer sauce to a small bowl. Season to taste with salt and pepper.

▶ Lightly oil grill rack and grill kebabs (covered only if using gas grill), turning occasionally, until tomatoes are softened, 2 to 3 minutes; zucchini is tender, 4 to 6 minutes; and lamb is medium-rare, about 6 minutes. Serve kebabs drizzled with sauce.

COOKS' NOTE: If you can't grill outdoors, cook the kebabs in batches on a lightly oiled two-burner ridged grill pan over moderately high heat. Grill the vegetables first, cooking the tomatoes for 6 to 8 minutes and the zucchini for 8 to 10 minutes. Transfer to a baking sheet as grilled and keep warm in a 200°F oven while grilling the lamb until medium-rare, 6 to 8 minutes.

Provençal Rack of Lamb with Roasted Tomatoes

Serves 2 | Active time: **30 minutes** | Start to finish: **50 minutes**

Rack of lamb, a popular restaurant cut, is easy to cook at home. Smaller Australian or New Zealand racks are the perfect size to serve two. Roasting the meat over sliced potatoes adds a savory kick.

- 2 **garlic cloves**
- ¾ **teaspoon salt**
- ¾ **teaspoon black pepper**
- 2 **teaspoons chopped fresh thyme**
- 1 **teaspoon chopped fresh rosemary**
- 3 **tablespoons olive oil**
- 2 **medium tomatoes, halved**
- 1 **(1-pound) frenched rack of lamb (4–8 chops, depending on size), cut in half**
- 2 **medium shallots, thinly sliced**
- 2 **medium boiling potatoes, peeled and sliced crosswise ¼ inch thick**
- 2 **tablespoons water**

SPECIAL SQUIPMENT
Instant-read thermometer

▶ Preheat oven to 400°F, with rack in middle.

▶ Mince and mash garlic to a paste with ½ teaspoon salt and ½ teaspoon pepper. Stir together with herbs and 1 tablespoon oil.

▶ Put tomatoes cut sides up in an oiled small baking dish and drizzle with one third of garlic mixture. Roast until tender, 30 to 40 minutes.

▶ Meanwhile, pat lamb dry and season with remaining ¼ teaspoon salt and remaining ¼ teaspoon pepper.

▶ Heat 1 tablespoon oil in a 10-inch oven-proof skillet over medium-high heat until it shimmers. Brown lamb on all sides, 4 to 6 minutes total. Transfer lamb to a cutting board and discard oil from skillet.

▶ Heat remaining tablespoon oil in skillet over medium heat and cook shallots and potatoes, stirring occasionally, until edges are browned, 3 to 5 minutes. Stir in water and half of remaining garlic mixture and remove from heat.

▶ Rub remaining garlic mixture on fat side of lamb racks. Arrange lamb over potatoes and roast in oven next to tomatoes until an instant-read thermometer inserted into center of meat (do not touch bone) registers 130°F for medium-rare, 20 to 25 minutes.

▶ Let stand, loosely covered, for 5 to 10 minutes. Serve with tomatoes.

< *Zucchini Carpaccio, page 168*

CHAPTER 9

SIDE DISHES

Think of these as your trustworthy allies, the dishes that have the power to transform a piece of meat or fish into a full-on dinner in no time flat. These sides bring drama and pacing to a meal, balancing other flavors and textures, supporting the main event. But take it from us, they're far from timid. Green beans tossed with ginger and garlic; sweet potatoes sprinkled with crisp fried sage leaves; paper-thin zucchini layered with Parmesan and mint: These are the dishes we secretly nibble when no one's looking—while waiting for guests to arrive, or, later, when we're alone in the kitchen tidying up. To us, they are the real stars.

Chopped Salad

Serves **10 to 12** | Active time: **45 minutes** | Start to finish: **1 hour**

This salad is great for picnics. It has all the components of a family favorite: beautiful color, satisfying crunch (courtesy of fresh zucchini, corn, and fennel), and a delicious dressing.

10 ounces frozen black-eyed peas (not thawed)
1 pound zucchini, trimmed
1 medium fennel bulb, stalks discarded
½ cup finely chopped scallions
2 tablespoons finely chopped fresh dill
3 tablespoons cider vinegar
2 tablespoons fresh lemon juice
1 tablespoon coarse-grain mustard
½ teaspoon black pepper
¼ teaspoon cayenne
2 tablespoons salt
⅓ cup extra-virgin olive oil
2¾ cups fresh corn (from about 4 ears)
1 pound frozen shelled edamame (not thawed)

▶ Bring 3 quarts water to a boil in a 5- to 6-quart pot, then cook black-eyed peas, partially covered, until tender, about 20 minutes.

▶ While peas are cooking, cut zucchini and fennel into ¼-inch dice. Whisk together scallions, dill, vinegar, lemon juice, mustard, black pepper, cayenne, and 1½ teaspoons salt in a large bowl. Add oil in a slow stream, whisking until emulsified. Add zucchini and fennel to dressing.

▶ When peas are tender, transfer with a slotted spoon to a sieve set over a large bowl, reserving cooking water in pot, and cool peas slightly, then add to salad.

▶ Return water to a boil and add remaining 1½ tablespoons salt, then cook corn and edamame, uncovered, until tender, 6 to 7 minutes. Transfer to sieve to cool slightly, then add to salad and stir to combine. Cool salad completely and serve chilled or at room temperature.

Asparagus with Feta

Serves 6 | **Active time: 10 minutes** | **Start to finish: 25 minutes**

How did we manage before we learned to roast asparagus? Don't get us wrong: Steamed asparagus spears are a classic. But roasting is just so easy; it concentrates the natural sweetness of the asparagus, here nicely balanced with the briny tang of feta.

2½ **pounds medium asparagus, trimmed**
2 **tablespoons extra-virgin olive oil**
½ **teaspoon salt**
¼ **teaspoon black pepper**
½ **cup crumbled feta**

▶ Preheat oven to 500°F, with rack in lower third.

▶ Toss asparagus with oil, salt, and pepper in a large rimmed baking sheet and arrange in one layer. Roast, shaking pan once about halfway through roasting, until asparagus is just tender when pierced with a fork, 8 to 14 minutes total.

▶ Transfer asparagus to a platter and sprinkle with cheese while still warm.

Ginger Garlic Green Beans

Serves **4** | Active time: **20 minutes** | Start to finish: **20 minutes**

1 **pound green beans, trimmed**
3 **garlic cloves**
  Salt
1 **tablespoon soy sauce**
1 **tablespoon grated peeled fresh**
  ginger
2 **teaspoons rice vinegar (not**
  seasoned)
1 **tablespoon vegetable oil**
½ **teaspoon Asian sesame oil**
1½ **teaspoons sesame seeds, toasted**

▶ Cook beans in a 6-quart pot of well-salted boiling water, uncovered, until just tender, 6 to 7 minutes. Drain in a colander, then plunge into an ice bath to stop cooking. Drain beans and pat dry.

▶ While beans cook, mince and mash garlic to a paste with a pinch of salt, then stir together with soy sauce, ginger, vinegar, and oils in a large bowl.

▶ Add beans and toss. Serve sprinkled with sesame seeds.

Green beans cooked crisp-tender retain their vivid color and snap, bringing freshness to the table no matter what the season. In this quick, Asian-inspired side, toasted sesame seeds—along with a dose of sesame oil—add an aromatic, nutty touch.

Broccoli with Hot Bacon Dressing

Serves **4** | Active time: **25 minutes** | Start to finish: **35 minutes**

Bacon, garlic, and raisins blend beautifully in a dish that's a welcome substitute for the basic broccoli-and-butter side.

2 **pounds broccoli, trimmed and cut into 1-inch florets (reserving stems)**

¼ **pound sliced bacon (about 4 slices), cut crosswise into ¼-inch-wide strips**

1 **garlic clove, finely chopped**

⅓ **cup raisins**

¼ **cup distilled white vinegar**

2 **tablespoons olive oil**

½ **teaspoon salt**

¼ **teaspoon black pepper**

▶ Peel broccoli stems with a vegetable peeler, then cut crosswise into ¼-inch slices.

▶ Cook bacon in a 12-inch heavy skillet over moderate heat, stirring occasionally, until browned and crisp, 4 to 5 minutes.

▶ Transfer bacon with a slotted spoon to several layers of paper towels to drain, leaving fat in skillet. Add garlic and raisins to skillet and cook over moderate heat, stirring, until garlic is pale golden, about 1 minute. Stir in vinegar, oil, salt, and pepper, then remove from heat.

▶ Meanwhile, cook broccoli florets and stems in a large pot of well-salted boiling water until just tender, 4 to 5 minutes. Drain broccoli well and transfer to a bowl.

▶ Bring dressing to a simmer, then cook, stirring, for 1 minute. Pour hot dressing over broccoli and sprinkle with bacon, tossing to combine.

Roasted Carrots with Thyme and Garlic

Adapted from April Bloomfield

Serves 4 | **Active time: 20 minutes** | **Start to finish: 1¼ hours**

An intense caramelization of the carrots concentrates their flavor and brings up their sweetness until they're almost like candy—but the roasted garlic and thyme keep the dish on the savory side.

- 2 tablespoons extra-virgin olive oil
- 2½ pounds large carrots, halved lengthwise diagonally
- 1 tablespoon unsalted butter
- 1 (2- to 3-inch) head of garlic, cloves separated but left unpeeled
- 3 sprigs thyme
- ¼ teaspoon Maldon sea salt
- ⅛ teaspoon black pepper
- ½ cup water

► Preheat oven to 400°F, with rack in middle position.

► Heat oil in a 12-inch heavy ovenproof skillet over moderately high heat until very hot and just beginning to smoke, then add half of carrots, cut sides down, and cook, undisturbed, until they begin to brown, 12 to 15 minutes. Transfer to a plate.

► Brown remaining carrots in same manner but leave in skillet. Add butter and stir once, then return carrots on plate to skillet. Continue to cook over moderately high heat, turning frequently, until carrots are golden brown on edges, about 5 minutes more.

► Add garlic, thyme, sea salt, pepper, and water and cover skillet tightly with foil. Roast in oven until carrots are tender, about 20 minutes.

► Remove foil and continue roasting, turning over carrots with tongs occasionally, until edges are slightly crisp, 10 to 15 minutes more.

KITCHEN TIP

THE PHYSICS OF ROASTING

Roasting is one of our favorite ways to prepare vegetables. The dry oven heat evaporates their juices, concentrating the natural sugars and other flavors. This process makes them insanely delicious, but also shrinks them considerably, so you need to buy more of a vegetable than you would if you were just going to steam it. In this recipe, 2½ pounds may seem like a lot for four people, but by the time they are finished in the oven, they'll have diminished in size—but increased exponentially in flavor.

Corn-and-Tomato Scramble

Serves 8 | Active time: **25 minutes** | Start to finish: **30 minutes**

Fresh corn and vine-ripened tomatoes taste best when prepared simply. Here, the corn is sautéed with scallions in butter, the tomatoes are lightly dressed with oil and cider vinegar, and then the two components are tossed together so that their flavors and juices mix into something new.

2 tablespoons extra-virgin olive oil
1 teaspoon cider vinegar
1½ teaspoons salt
¾ teaspoon black pepper
1¼ pounds tomatoes, cut into bite-size pieces
1 bunch scallions, finely chopped, keeping white parts and greens separate
2 tablespoons unsalted butter
4 cups corn kernels (from about 8 ears)

▶ Whisk together oil, vinegar, ¾ teaspoon salt, and ¼ teaspoon pepper. Toss tomatoes with dressing.
▶ While tomatoes marinate, cook white parts of scallions in butter with ¾ teaspoon salt and ½ teaspoon pepper in a 12-inch heavy skillet over medium-high heat, stirring occasionally, until golden, about 4 minutes. Add corn and sauté until just tender, about 5 minutes. Transfer to a bowl and cool.
▶ Stir together corn mixture, tomatoes, and scallion greens.

COOKS' NOTE: The corn can be cooked 1 day ahead and chilled. Bring to room temperature before using.

KITCHEN TIP
FARM-STAND INTELLIGENCE

Searching for the perfect tomato? Sniff it: Ripe tomatoes have an astringent, green-vine fragrance. Sample from the full range of colors available, and stay away from greenhouse tomatoes if sun-ripened are available. Chilling tomatoes kills their flavor and turns their texture to cotton. Do not put them in the refrigerator. Ever.

Panfried Smashed Potatoes

Serves **4** | Active time: **10 minutes** | Start to finish: **45 minutes**

These are everything potatoes should be: crisp-skinned yet pillowy, generously sprinkled with salty Parmesan. And no peeling required!

- 8 **medium red potatoes (about 2 inches long; 1¾ pounds)**
- 1 **tablespoon salt**
- ½ **cup extra-virgin olive oil**
- ½ **cup grated Parmigiano-Reggiano**
  Black pepper

▶ Generously cover potatoes with cold water in a 3- to 4-quart pot and add salt. Boil until almost tender, 10 to 15 minutes. Drain potatoes. Transfer to a baking sheet and lightly crush to about ¾-inch thick with a potato masher, keeping potatoes intact as much as possible.

▶ Heat oil in a 12-inch heavy skillet over medium-high heat until it shimmers. Transfer potatoes with a spatula to skillet, then lower heat to medium-low and cook, turning once, until golden brown, about 20 minutes total.

▶ Sprinkle with cheese, season generously with pepper, and serve.

COOKS' NOTE: The fried potatoes can be kept warm on a baking sheet in a 200°F oven for up to 30 minutes.

Sweet Potatoes with Sage

Serves 8 | Active time: **25 minutes** | Start to finish: **1 hour**

In this autumnal side dish, garlic oil "savorizes" sweet potatoes gently caramelized in the oven. Fried sage leaves are a lovely garnish.

FOR SWEET POTATOES
- 3 **large garlic cloves**
- ¼ **cup olive oil**
- ¾ **teaspoon salt**
- 2½ **pounds sweet potatoes, peeled and sliced into ½-inch-thick rounds**

FOR FRIED SAGE
- ⅓ **cup olive oil**
- 24 **fresh sage leaves**

▶ **ROAST SWEET POTATOES:** Preheat oven to 450°F, with rack in upper third.

▶ Puree garlic with oil and salt in a blender until smooth. Toss sweet potatoes with garlic oil in a large bowl, then spread in one layer in a 15-by-10-inch rimmed baking sheet.

▶ Bake until golden in patches and cooked through, 20 to 30 minutes.

▶ **FRY SAGE LEAVES:** Heat oil in a small heavy skillet over medium-high heat until it shimmers, then fry sage leaves in 2 batches, stirring, until crisp, 30 seconds to 1 minute per batch. Transfer with a slotted spoon to paper towels to drain.

▶ Serve sweet potatoes with sage leaves scattered on top.

COOKS' NOTES: The sweet potatoes can be cut and tossed with garlic oil 4 hours ahead and chilled in a sealable bag.

The sage leaves can be fried 4 hours ahead and kept at room temperature.

Zucchini Carpaccio

Serves 4 to 6 | **Active time: 15 minutes** | **Start to finish: 15 minutes**

A few humble ingredients—paper-thin slices of raw zucchini drizzled with lemon juice and olive oil and sprinkled with Parmigiano and fresh mint—equal perfection on a plate.

4   **medium zucchini (1¼ pounds total)**
¼   **cup extra-virgin olive oil**
1½   **tablespoons fresh lemon juice, or to taste**
½   **teaspoon salt, or to taste**
⅓–½ **cup grated Parmigiano-Reggiano**
¼–⅓ **cup fresh mint leaves**

SPECIAL EQUIPMENT
   Mandoline or other adjustable-blade slicer; scissors

▶ Cut zucchini crosswise into slices as thin as possible with mandoline and spread them out evenly on a large platter (or use two large plates), covering platter completely.

▶ Drizzle zucchini evenly with oil and lemon juice, then sprinkle evenly with salt and cheese. Using scissors, snip thin shreds of the mint leaves over the salad.

KITCHEN TIP
A HOST'S BEST FRIEND

This dish would be right at home as part of an anti-pasto spread or arranged on individual plates for a very snazzy—and easy—first course. It's a boon to the host, because it's just as delicious when freshly made as it is after sitting for an hour or two, when the zucchini has wilted and softened, allowing the mint, Parmigiano, and lemon vinaigrette to mingle. Do yourself a favor and don't scrimp on these few ingredients: Use the freshest, firmest zucchini, the sweetest mint, and real Parmigiano-Reggiano.

< *Chocolate*
Fallen
Soufflé Cake,
page 180

CHAPTER 10

DESSERTS

We could have subtitled this chapter "the sweet spot," because everything in it inhabits that magic zone where the pleasure of making and the pleasure of eating intersect. In other words, these recipes are as easy as they are delicious. And while nutritionists may not see dessert as necessary, to us pleasure is a daily requirement, and these dishes are as essential as any in our collection. We all need a handful of sure-fire, go-to treats we can whip up quickly when the occasion (or the hankering) calls for it. The ones we've collected here are sure to please a crowd—and to disappear fast. When it comes to milk chocolate pudding or blackberry peach cobbler, there's no need to remind anyone to "save room for dessert." The hunger will appear the moment you set them on the table.

Peaches Under Meringue

Serves 4 | **Active time: 10 minutes** | **Start to finish: 10 minutes**

What could be simpler? Crown broiled peaches with pillows of meringue and a bit of honeyed crunch for one of our favorite quick desserts.

2 ripe peaches, halved and pitted
3 tablespoons plus 1 teaspoon sugar
1 large egg white
  Salt
2 tablespoons finely chopped sesame candy or crushed amaretti

▶ Preheat broiler.
▶ Put peaches, cut side up, on a baking sheet and sprinkle with 1 teaspoon sugar. Broil 4 to 5 inches from heat until tops begin to brown, 2 to 4 minutes. Remove sheet from broiler.
▶ Beat egg white with a pinch of salt in a small deep bowl using an electric mixer at medium-high speed until foamy. Gradually add remaining 3 tablespoons sugar, beating until white holds stiff, glossy peaks. Fold in sesame candy.
▶ Place a dollop of meringue on each peach half and broil for 30 seconds. Turn off broiler and leave peaches in oven just until tips of meringue are browned, 30 seconds to 1 minute (watch carefully).

COOKS' NOTE: The egg white in this recipe is not fully cooked.

Fruit-on-the-Bottom Tapioca Pudding

Serves 6 | **Active time: 15 minutes** | **Start to finish: 40 minutes**

Beneath a creamy layer of tapioca pudding lurks a silky strawberry base. Ground fennel seeds perk up the flavor of the fruit.

2 cups water
⅓ cup small tapioca pearls
1 cup heavy cream
6 tablespoons sugar
⅛ teaspoon salt
1 teaspoon fennel seeds
1 quart strawberries, trimmed and coarsely chopped

SPECIAL EQUIPMENT
Electric coffee/spice grinder or mortar and pestle

▶ Bring water to a boil in a 1-quart heavy saucepan. Whisk in tapioca and simmer, uncovered, whisking until mostly translucent, about 15 minutes. Whisk in cream, ¼ cup sugar, and salt and simmer, uncovered, whisking until tapioca is cooked through, about 3 minutes. Transfer to a metal bowl and set in an ice bath to cool, stirring until thickened.

▶ Meanwhile, grind fennel seeds in grinder. Pulse strawberries in a food processor with fennel and remaining 2 tablespoons sugar until coarsely pureed. Divide among 6-ounce glasses.

▶ Spoon tapioca over strawberries. Chill until cold, at least 15 minutes.

COOKS' NOTE: The dessert can be made 1 day ahead and chilled, covered. The tapioca will continue to thicken and set as it chills. If desired, let sit at room temperature for 20 to 30 minutes to soften slightly.

Apple Upside-Down Cornmeal Cakes

Serves 6 | Active time: **25 minutes** | Start to finish: **45 minutes**

You may want to double this recipe—the apple-walnut topping and whipped cream make these quick-cooking cakes disappear fast.

6   **tablespoons (¾ stick) cold unsalted butter, cut into tablespoons, plus additional for greasing**
3   **Gala apples**
⅓   **cup packed light brown sugar**
1   **teaspoon fresh lemon juice**
½   **cup coarsely chopped walnuts**
¾   **cup all-purpose flour**
½   **cup yellow cornmeal**
⅓   **cup granulated sugar**
2   **teaspoons baking powder**
¼   **teaspoon salt**
1   **large egg**
¾   **cup whole milk**

SPECIAL EQUIPMENT
   Muffin pan with 6 (1-cup) muffin cups

ACCOMPANIMENT
   Lightly sweetened whipped cream

▶ Preheat oven to 425°F, with rack in upper third. Butter muffin cups.

▶ Peel and core apples, then cut into ⅓-inch dice. Heat 2 tablespoons butter in a 12-inch heavy skillet over moderate heat until foam subsides, then cook apples, brown sugar, and lemon juice, stirring occasionally, until liquid is reduced to a glaze and apples are tender, 5 to 6 minutes.

▶ Stir in walnuts and divide apple mixture among muffin cups.

▶ Pulse together flour, cornmeal, granulated sugar, baking powder, and salt in a food processor until combined. Add remaining 4 tablespoons butter and pulse until mixture resembles coarse meal with some small (roughly pea-size) butter lumps.

▶ Whisk together egg and milk in a large bowl. Add flour mixture and whisk until just combined.

▶ Divide batter among muffin cups and bake until golden and a wooden pick or skewer inserted into center of a cake comes out clean, 15 to 20 minutes.

▶ Run a paring knife around edge of each cake to loosen. Invert rack over muffin cups, then invert cakes onto rack. Serve warm with a dollop of whipped cream.

Blackberry Peach Cobbler

Serves 12 | Active time: **25 minutes** | Start to finish: **1½ hours**

We recommend baking this luscious cobbler ahead of time—that way you can reheat it while clearing the table. Otherwise you can just whisk together the dry ingredients beforehand, but you'll have to excuse yourself during dinner to assemble and bake the dessert.

- 2 **tablespoons cornstarch**
- 1½ **cups plus 1 teaspoon sugar**
- 1¼ **pounds blackberries (5 cups)**
- 2 **pounds peaches (6 medium), peeled (see Cooks' Notes), pitted, and cut into ½-inch-thick wedges**
- 3 **cups all-purpose flour**
- 1 **tablespoon baking powder**
- 1 **teaspoon salt**
- 16 **tablespoons (2 sticks) cold unsalted butter, cut into ½-inch cubes**
- 1 **cup plus 3 tablespoons whole milk**

▶ Preheat oven to 425°F, with rack in middle. Butter a 13-by-9-by-2-inch glass or ceramic baking dish (3-quart capacity).

▶ Whisk together cornstarch and 1½ cups sugar in a large bowl, then add blackberries and peaches and toss to combine well. Transfer to baking dish and bake until just bubbling, 10 to 15 minutes.

▶ While fruit bakes, whisk together flour, baking powder, and salt in another large bowl, then blend in butter with your fingertips or a pastry blender until mixture resembles coarse meal. Add milk and stir just until a dough forms. (Dough will be sticky.)

▶ Drop dough onto hot fruit mixture in 12 mounds (about ⅓ cup each), then sprinkle dough with remaining teaspoon sugar. Bake cobbler until top is golden, 25 to 35 minutes. Serve warm.

COOKS' NOTES: To peel the peaches, first cut an X in the end opposite the stem and immerse in a large pot of boiling water, 3 at a time, for 15 seconds. Transfer with a slotted spoon to an ice bath and then peel.

The cobbler can be baked 6 hours ahead and cooled completely, uncovered, then chilled, covered. Before serving, let stand at room temperature for 1 hour, then reheat in a preheated 350°F oven until warm, about 20 minutes.

KITCHEN TIP

EASY DOES IT

A cobbler is the perfect thing to make if you're entertaining guests for the weekend, because it can just sit on a counter, waiting for someone to come along and take some. (Leftovers, drizzled with heavy cream, are grand for breakfast.) The cobbler here—full of sweet, golden peaches and the purple tartness of blackberries—is particularly easy to throw together because you don't have to fuss with rolling out pastry or biscuit dough. Just plop the biscuits down on top of the piping-hot filling; that way the underside of the dough cooks through completely, and the topping will be tender and fluffy.

Dutch Baby
with Lemon Sugar

Serves 4 to 6 | **Active time: 10 minutes** | **Start to finish: 30 minutes**

The Dutch baby—basically a cross between a pancake and a popover—is tremendously popular in Seattle. According to local lore, it originated at a restaurant there called Manca's. Serve this one with fresh berries or nothing more than jam or a lavish sprinkling of lemon sugar.

⅓ **cup sugar**

2 **teaspoons grated lemon zest**

3 **large eggs at room temperature for 30 minutes**

⅔ **cup whole milk at room temperature**

⅔ **cup all-purpose flour**

¼ **teaspoon vanilla extract**

⅛ **teaspoon ground cinnamon**

⅛ **teaspoon grated nutmeg**

⅛ **teaspoon salt**

4 **tablespoons (½ stick) unsalted butter, cut into pieces**

SPECIAL EQUIPMENT
10-inch cast-iron skillet

ACCOMPANIMENT
Lemon wedges

▶ Put skillet on middle rack of oven and preheat oven to 450°F.

▶ Stir together sugar and zest in a small bowl.

▶ Beat eggs with an electric mixer at high speed until pale and frothy, then beat in milk, flour, vanilla, cinnamon, nutmeg, and salt and continue to beat until smooth, about 1 minute more (batter will be thin).

▶ Add butter to hot skillet and melt, swirling to coat. Add batter and immediately return skillet to oven. Bake until puffed and golden brown, 18 to 25 minutes.

▶ Serve immediately, topped with lemon sugar, with lemon wedges alongside.

Chocolate Fallen Soufflé Cake

Serves **8 to 10** | Active time: **30 minutes** | Start to finish: **3 hours**

Call it chocolate bliss: A crackly crust gives way to a tender, melt-in-the mouth, bittersweet center. If you're not familiar with soufflé cakes, this dessert may look a little odd at first; it's meant to be eaten once it has collapsed and cooled (just the opposite of a regular soufflé).

12   **ounces fine-quality bittersweet chocolate, chopped**

12   **tablespoons (1½ sticks) unsalted butter, cut into tablespoons**

1½   **teaspoon vanilla extract**
     Salt

¾   **cup sugar**

5   **large eggs, separated and at room temperature for 30 minutes**

¼   **cup all-purpose flour**

ACCOMPANIMENT
    Ice cream or lightly sweetened whipped cream

▶ Preheat oven to 350°F, with rack in middle. Butter a 9-inch springform pan and line bottom with a round of parchment or wax paper, then butter paper.

▶ Melt chocolate and butter in a large metal bowl set over a pan of barely simmering water (or in a large microwave-safe bowl in a microwave at 50 percent power for 4 to 5 minutes), stirring frequently, then cool completely. Whisk in vanilla, ¼ teaspoon salt, and 6 tablespoons sugar. Add yolks 1 at a time, whisking well after each addition. Whisk in flour.

▶ Beat whites with a pinch of salt in a bowl using an electric mixer at medium-high speed until they hold soft peaks, then add remaining 6 tablespoons sugar a little at a time, beating, and continue to beat until whites hold stiff glossy peaks.

▶ Whisk about one fourth of whites into chocolate mixture to lighten, then fold in remaining whites gently but thoroughly. Pour batter into springform pan, spreading evenly.

▶ Bake until a wooden pick or skewer inserted in center comes out with moist crumbs adhering, 35 to 40 minutes.

▶ Cool cake in pan on a rack for 10 minutes. Remove side of pan and cool cake completely. Invert cake onto rack and remove bottom of pan, discarding paper, then invert cake onto a plate. Serve with ice cream or whipped cream.

COOKS' NOTE: The cake (removed from the pan) can be made 1 day ahead and kept, wrapped in plastic wrap, at room temperature.

KITCHEN TIP
MAKING A PERFECT SOUFFLÉ CAKE

The success of this cake rests on properly beaten egg whites that are correctly folded into the batter. Begin by separating the eggs when they're cold, because the yolks are less likely to break. Then let the yolks and whites come to room temperature; the whites don't expand as well when cold. To give the beaten whites more stability, we slowly add some sugar once they hold soft peaks and then beat the whites to stiff, glossy peaks. (It's best to err on the side of not-quite-there rather than risk overbeating them.) Finally, to combine the beaten egg whites with the much heavier chocolate batter without losing too much volume, you first lighten the batter by stirring in a portion of the whites, then gently fold in the remainder. That's it—easy!

Milk Chocolate Pudding

Serves 4 to 6 | **Active time: 15 minutes** | Start to finish: **2¼ hours (includes chilling)**

Move over, bittersweet: Milk chocolate's satisfyingly smooth, creamy texture and gentler profile is on full nostalgic display in this classic pudding.

2 **tablespoons sugar**
2 **tablespoons cornstarch**
2 **tablespoons unsweetened cocoa powder**
 Salt
1½ **cups whole milk**
½ **cup heavy cream**
4 **ounces fine-quality milk chocolate, chopped**
1 **teaspoon vanilla extract**
ACCOMPANIMENT
 Lightly sweetened whipped cream

▶ Whisk together sugar, cornstarch, cocoa powder, and a pinch of salt in a 2-quart heavy saucepan, then gradually whisk in milk and cream. Bring to a boil over moderately high heat, whisking constantly, then boil, whisking, for 2 minutes. (Mixture will be thick.) Remove from heat. Whisk in chocolate and vanilla until smooth.

▶ Transfer to a bowl and chill pudding, its surface covered with wax paper (to prevent a skin from forming), until cold, at least 2 hours. Serve with whipped cream.

COOKS' NOTES: The pudding can be chilled, covered with plastic wrap after 2 hours, for up to 3 days.

If you're short on time, you can quick-chill the pudding by putting it in a metal bowl and then setting it in an ice bath, stirring frequently until cold, about 15 minutes. Replenish the ice as necessary.

Chocolate Caramel Sauce

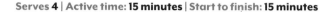

Serves **4** | Active time: **15 minutes** | Start to finish: **15 minutes**

½ **cup sugar**
¾ **cup heavy cream**
4 **ounces fine-quality bittersweet chocolate, coarsely chopped**
⅛ **teaspoon salt**
½ **teaspoon vanilla extract**
ACCOMPANIMENT
1 **quart vanilla or coffee ice cream**

► Cook sugar in a dry heavy medium saucepan over moderately high heat, undisturbed, until sugar begins to melt, 1 to 2 minutes. Continue to cook, stirring occasionally with a fork (sugar will form clumps but eventually melt), until sugar is completely melted into a deep golden caramel, 2 to 3 minutes.

► Remove caramel from heat and carefully pour in cream (mixture will steam and bubble vigorously and caramel will harden). Once bubbles begin to subside, return pan to moderately low heat and cook, stirring, until caramel is dissolved. Remove from heat, then add chocolate and salt and stir until sauce is smooth. Stir in vanilla. Cool sauce to warm and serve over ice cream in bowls.

Two dynamic flavors combine winningly in this easy sauce, providing delicious proof that the whole is greater than the sum of its parts.

MENUS

September Farmers' Market Dinner

Peaches with Serrano Ham and Basil
(page 15)

Porterhouse Steak with Pan-Seared Cherry Tomatoes
(page 138)

Panfried Smashed Potatoes
(page 164)

Zucchini Carpaccio
(page 168)

Arugula Salad

Peaches Under Meringue
(page 172)

Miner Viognier, California ($11):
A classic bouquet with stone fruits and florals, a voluptuous palate, and a dry finish. A great cooler-weather white.

Querciabella Mongrana, Maremma, Italy ($15):
This wine sings when paired with steak and tomatoes.

Kracher Auslese Cuvée , Neusiedlersee, Austria ($19):
The Neusiedlersee region produces some of the world's great dessert wines. This one has enough zippy acidity to lift your guests through the end of the meal.

Pool Party

Chile Peanuts
(page 14)

Tomato and Tomatillo Gazpacho
(page 34)

Lobster Rolls with Lemon Vinaigrette and Garlic Butter
(page 52)

Barbecued Pork Burgers with Slaw
(page 60)

Chopped Salad
(page 154)

Tossed Green Salad

Fruit-on-the-Bottom Tapioca Pudding
(page 173)

Agapé Crémant d'Alsace NV ($19):
The savvy shopper's alternative to pricey Champagne: same grape varietals, same method, great creamy flavor, and looks great in the glass.

Leitz Riesling Rüdesheimer Klosterlay Kabinett, Rheingau, Germany ($15):
A serious wine from a serious producer in a serious region at a not-so-serious price. Juicy fruit balanced with slatey minerality and a bright acidity.

Tres Picos Borsao, Campo de Borja, Spain ($12):
A perfect poolside red. Fruity, a little spicy.

Elegant Dinner Party

Buckwheat Pancakes with Smoked Salmon
(page 24)

Herb-Roasted Pork Loin
(page 144)

Roasted Carrots with Thyme and Garlic
(page 160)

Steamed Green Beans with Lemon Butter

Endive Salad

Chocolate Fallen Soufflé Cake
(page 180)

Schramsberg Mirabelle Rosé Brut, Napa ($20):
A dry *méthode champenoise* rosé is a sophisticated starter (and if you want to drink it all the way through the meal, you won't regret it).

Cadence Coda, Red Mountain, Washington ($20):
This cool Washington State region is producing genteel and graceful Bordeaux-style blends that will wow without breaking the bank.

Smith Woodhouse Lodge Reserve Port ($18):
A nonvintage bottling that spends five years in cask. A decadent accompaniment to the chocolate soufflé cake.

Mexican Grill

Mexican Seafood Cocktail
(page 26)

Grilled Skirt Steaks with Tomatillos Two Ways
(page 140)

Warm Tortillas

Orange and Avocado Salad

Milk Chocolate Pudding
(page 182)

Loimer Grüner Veltliner "Lois," Kamptal, Austria ($12):
A fresh, crisp, peppery white that handles seafood, vegetables, and spice beautifully.

Substance Cabernet Franc, Washington ($19):
The characteristic leafy, sappy character of Cabernet Franc is a great match for the tomatillos that accompany the skirt steaks.

Vietti Moscato d'Asti, Piedmont, Italy ($13):
This gently sweet sparkler can be enjoyed before, during, and after the meal.

Date Night

Goat Cheese with Olives,
Lemon, and Thyme
(page 16)

Provençal Rack of Lamb
with Roasted Tomatoes
(page 150)

Dutch Baby
with Lemon Sugar
(page 178)

**Mulderbosch Sauvignon
Blanc, Stellenbosch,
South Africa ($14):**
A twist on the traditional Loire
Valley pairing of Sancerre or
Pouilly-Fumé with goat cheese.

**Domaine de Triennes St.
Auguste, Provence ($14):**
The harmonious blend of
Cabernet Sauvignon, Merlot,
and Syrah is a slam dunk for the
menu's Provençal flavors. What
grows together goes together.

**Baumard Quarts de Chaume,
Loire, France ($22 for 375 ml):**
From a top producer of Chenin
Blanc, this golden, sweet
Loire Valley wine is a tongue-
coating elixir.

Sunday Night
Fireside Supper

Winter Minestrone
(page 42)

Grilled Cheese with
Onion Jam, Taleggio,
and Escarole
(page 48)

Apple Upside-Down
Cornmeal Cakes
(page 174)

**Palmina Arneis, Santa Ynez,
California ($18):**
This Central Coast white displays
lime, pear, and honey notes—a
pumped-up version of the
Piemontese original.

**Paul Jaboulet Côtes du
Rhône Parallèle 45 ($10):**
This blend of Syrah and
Grenache has been a standby
and steal for years.

Thanksgiving
Eve Open House

Garlic and
Cheese Crostini
(page 20)

Portuguese Kale
and Potato Soup
(page 38)

Pinto Bean Mole Chili
(page 96)

Romaine Salad

Ice Cream with
Chocolate Caramel Sauce
(page 183)

**Sokol Blosser Pinot Gris,
Willamette Valley,
Oregon ($18):**
A fleshy, brown-spiced aromatic
white from one of the Oregon
wine industry's founding
families.

**Delta Pinot Noir,
Marlborough,
New Zealand ($20):**
A distinctive red-fruited example
of the cool-climate Pinots from
the South Island of New Zealand.

**Tikal Patriota, Mendoza,
Argentina ($18):**
Black and red berry fruit with
cocoa and vanilla.

Summer
House Dinner

Roasted-Tomato Tart
(page 22)

Zucchini-Basil Soup
(page 40)

Grilled Herbed
Poussins
(page 134)

Corn-and-Tomato
Scramble
(page 162)

Roasted New Potatoes

Blackberry Peach Cobbler
(page 176)

**Marcel Deiss Pinot Blanc,
Alsace, France ($16):**
Citrus, honey, peach—summer in
a glass.

**Hippolyte Reverdy Sancerre
Rouge, Loire, France ($20):**
This elegant Pinot Noir is a
revelation and a great refresher,
especially when served with a
hint of chill.

**Lini Lambrusco Rosato,
Emilia-Romagna, Italy ($16):**
This Lambrusco echoes the berry
fruits in the cobbler.

Credits

RECIPES AND TEXT
Andrea Albin, Celia Barbour, Lillian Chou, Kay Chun, Ruth Cousineau, Gina Marie Miraglia Eriquez, Paul Grimes, Ian Knauer, Jane Daniels Lear, Amy Mastrangelo, Kemp Minifie, Lori Powell, Melissa Roberts, Maggie Ruggiero, Zanne Stewart, Alexis M. Touchet, John Willoughby, Shelton Wiseman

MENUS
Pages 184–85: Kemp Minifie

WINES NOTES
Pages 184–85: by Belinda Chang, General Manager and Wine Director of New York's The Monkey Bar

BOOK DESIGN
Margaret Swart

PHOTOGRAPHY
Cover: John Kernick; food styling by Paul Grimes
Quentin Bacon: page 163
Roland Bello: pages 125, 145
Stephanie Foley: page 53
Matthew Hranek: page 29
Ditte Isager: page 169
John Kernick: pages 19, 34, 67, 71, 73, 138, 161, 167
Geoff Lung: page 177
Marcus Nilsson: pages 49, 111, 133
Jeffrey Schad and Chris Gentile: pages 12, 30, 46, 62, 82, 100, 118, 136, 152, 170
Mikkel Vang: pages 15, 37, 135
Anna Williams: page 181
Romulo Yanes: pages 14, 15, 21, 23, 25, 27, 33, 35, 39, 41, 43, 45, 51, 55, 57, 59 61, 65, 69, 75, 77, 79, 81, 85, 87, 89, 91–92, 93, 95, 97, 99, 103, 105, 107, 109, 113, 115, 117, 121, 123, 127, 129, 131, 139, 141, 143, 147, 149, 151, 155–57, 159, 165, 172–73, 175, 179, 182–183

GOURMET SPECIAL EDITIONS
Executive Director, Content Development Catherine Kelley
Design Directors Wyatt Mitchell and Alyson Keeling Cameron
Food Editor Kemp Minifie
Editorial Systems Director Kristen Rayner
Director of Studios Jeffrey Schad
Studio Coordinator Jesse Newhouse

CONDÉ NAST PUBLICATIONS
Editorial Director Thomas J. Wallace
Senior Vice President, Editorial Operations Rick Levine
Vice-President, Digital Magazine Development Scott Dadich

SPECIAL THANKS
Christine Arzeno
Belinda Chang
Christopher Donnellan
Michelle Egan
Rose Gold
Christopher Jagger
James Mate
Julie Michalowski
Clare O'Shea
Pamela Duncan Silver
Mariana Velasquez
Alden Wallace

INDEX

A

ancho chiles, 96
anchovy sauce, spicy, pasta with dill
    bread crumbs and, 68
angel-hair pasta (capellini), 66
    with fresh tomato sauce, 66
    with salmon and lemon-dill-vodka
        sauce, 72
appetizers, *see* snacks and starters
apple upside-down cornmeal cakes, 174
Asian flavors:
    bacon-and-egg rice, 80
    ginger garlic green beans, 157
    Korean-style grilled flank steak, 139
    sticky sesame chicken wings, 122
    see also Vietnamese flavors
asparagus:
    with feta, 156
    and morel ragout, risotto with, 78

B

bacon:
    BLT burgers, 54
    dressing, hot, broccoli with, 158
    -and-egg rice, 80
baking pans, 10
banh mi, 58
barbecued pork burgers with slaw, 60
basil:
    angel-hair pasta with fresh tomato
        sauce, 66
    inside-out eggplant Parmigiana
        stack, 93–94
    peaches with serrano ham and, 15
    zucchini soup, 40
bean(s):
    black-, burgers, 50
    black-eyed peas, Greek salad with
        orzo and, 88
    black-eyed peas, in chopped salad,
        154
    cannellini, in winter minestrone, 42
    chickpea-potato masala, rava dosas
        with, 90–92
    pinto, mole chili, 96
    refried, in chicken tostadas, 120
    white-, stew, fast, 35
bean thread noodles, in summer rolls
        with sweet-and-savory dipping
        sauce, 86

beef, 137–40
    BLT burgers, 54
    flank steak, Korean-style grilled, 139
    porterhouse steak with pan-seared
        cherry tomatoes, 138
    skirt steaks, grilled, with tomatillos
        two ways, 140
    sophisto joes, 56
beurre blanc (butter sauce), tarragon, 114
black-bean burgers, 50
blackberry peach cobbler, 176
black-eyed peas:
    chopped salad, 154
    Greek salad with orzo and, 88
black pepper, 10
BLT burgers, 54
bread crumbs:
    dill, pasta with spicy anchovy sauce
        and, 68
    panko, for crispiest coating, 124
broccoli rabe crostini, 18
broccoli with hot bacon dressing, 158
bruschetta, grilled eggplant and
        smoked-Gouda, 84
buckwheat pancakes with smoked
        salmon, 24
burgers, 47
    barbecued pork, with slaw, 60
    black-bean, 50
    BLT, 54
butternut squash:
    chopping, 36
    curried squash and red-lentil soup, 36
butter sauce (beurre blanc), tarragon, 114

C

cakes:
    apple upside-down cornmeal, 174
    chocolate fallen soufflé, 180
cannellini beans:
    fast white-bean stew, 35
    winter minestrone, 42
capellini, *see* angel-hair pasta
caper sauce, 142
caramel sauce, chocolate, 183
carrots:
    roasted, with thyme and garlic, 160
    sweet-and-sour chicken thighs with,
        126
cheese(s):
    cheesy chicken and mushroom
        lasagne, 76

and garlic crostini, 20
    grilled, with onion jam, Taleggio, and
        escarole, 48
    Mexican, 120
    smoked-, and grilled eggplant
        bruschetta, 84
    see also feta; Parmigiano-Reggiano
chicken, 119–32
    banh mi, 58
    breasts, grilled, with yogurt sauce
        and mint salad, 128
    drumsticks, deviled, 124
    meatballs, baked, with peperonata,
        130
    and mushroom lasagne, cheesy, 76
    removing backbone of, 132
    in Riesling, 132
    thighs, sweet-and-sour, with carrots,
        126
    tostadas, 120
    wings, sticky sesame, 122
chickpea-potato masala, rava dosas
        with, 90–92
chile(s), 11
    ancho and chipotle, 96
    peanuts, 14
chili, pinto bean mole, 96
chipotle chiles, 96
chocolate:
    caramel sauce, 183
    fallen soufflé cake, 180
    melting, 10
    milk, pudding, 182
chopped salad, 154
chowder, shellfish, 44
citrus:
    yogurt sauce, 104
    zest, 11
cobbler, blackberry peach, 176
coconut, in Indian shrimp curry, 112
cookware, nonreactive, 10
corn:
    chopped salad, 154
    -and-tomato scramble, 162
cornmeal:
    cakes, apple upside-down, 174
    shrimp and pancetta on polenta, 110
cotija cheese (queso añejo), 120
crabmeat:
    Mexican seafood cocktail, 26
    shellfish chowder, 44
crema, Mexican, 120
crispness, secret to, 124